TRADE UNION
GROWTH AND DECLINE

TRADE UNION GROWTH AND DECLINE

An International Study

WALTER GALENSON

Westport, Connecticut
London

The following have generously given permission to use extended quotations from copy-righted works: American Economic Association; Blackwell Publishers; *British Journal of Industrial Relations*; Gary N. Chaison; Croom Helm; Les Éditions Ouvrières; Richard Freeman; The Gallup Organization; HarperCollins Publishers; Industrial Relations Research Association; Johns Hopkins University Press; *Journal of Labor Research*; Macmillan; Organization for Economic Co-operation and Development, Paris; Oxford University Press; Queen's University; Routledge; Sage Publications Ltd.; Solar Foundation of Bombay; University of Wisconsin Press; Unwin Hyman; Wharton School; World Bank; Zed Books.

Library of Congress Cataloging-in-Publication Data

Galenson, Walter.
  Trade union growth and decline : an international study / Walter Galenson.
    p.   cm.
  Includes bibliographical references and index.
  ISBN 0-275-94325-9
  1. Trade unions—Membership—History—20th century. 2. Trade unions—United States—Membership—History—20th century.
  I. Title.
  HD6476.G273   1994
  331.87'32'0973—dc20   93-40199

British Library Cataloguing in Publication Data is available.

Library of Congress Catalog Card Number: 93-40199
ISBN: 0-275-94325-9

First published in 1994

Praeger Publishers, 88 Post Road West, Westport, CT 06881
An imprint of Greenwood Publishing Group, Inc.

Printed in the United States of America

The paper used in this book complies with the Permanent Paper Standard issued by the National Information Standards Organization (Z39.48—1984).

10 9 8 7 6 5 4 3 2 1

For Marjorie

Contents

CHAPTER 1

Trade Union Membership

The decline in the unionized portion of the U.S. labor force during the past 25 years has occasioned much comment. Many of those who have examined the causes regard the decline as largely an American phenomenon. For example, Richard Freeman wrote in *The Journal of Economic Perspectives,* "Even read cautiously [the data] clearly contradict the notion that the decline in union density in the United States is part of a general collapse of unions in the developed world; in most countries, union density increased in the 1970s and stabilized or declined modestly in the 1980s at levels above those in earlier years. . . . Overall, the patterns of change . . . highlight the fact that de-unionization is largely, if not exclusively, a U.S. development."[1]

Data for recent years indicate that the U.S. decline, while steeper than in most other countries, is part of a phenomenon that has affected almost all industrial nations and many less developed countries as well. During most of the twentieth century, union membership tended to rise in most countries, although with interruptions because of political and economic events. During the 1980s, and even earlier in many parts of the world, the density of union membership has dropped, often under relatively favorable conditions.

Many factors have been adduced to explain the reversal in the fortunes of the U.S. labor movement, although less attention has been paid to similar developments in other countries, excepting Great Britain. A less ethnocentric approach to the question may be more fruitful, because similar causal factors may be found to prevail elsewhere.

Until recently, comparative union membership data were difficult to obtain. The gap was filled by a study of union density in the countries

Table 1.1
Trade Union Density: Industrial Countries (Union Membership as a Percentage of Employed Wage and Salary Workers)

	1980	1988	1980-1988
Australia	49.0[a]	42.0	-14.3
Canada	35.1	34.6	- 1.4
Denmark	76.5	73.2	- 4.3
France	19.0	12.0	-36.8
Germany	37.0	33.8	- 8.6
Italy	49.3	39.6	-19.7
Japan	31.1	26.8	-13.8
New Zealand	55.0	42.1[b]	-23.5
Norway	56.9	57.1[c]	+ 0.4
Spain	22.0	16.0[d]	-27.3
Sweden	80.0	85.3	+ 6.6
United Kingdom	50.7	41.5	-18.1
United States	23.0	16.4[c]	-28.7

Source: Jelle Visser, "Trends in Union Membership," OECD, *Employment Outlook,* Paris, July 1991, p. 101.
[a]1982; [b]1990; [c]1989; [d]1985-1990.

that belong to the Organization for Economic Cooperation and Development (OECD) that used a uniform and sophisticated methodology (see figures in Table 1.1).[2] More recently, the U.S. Bureau of Labor Statistics (BLS) did a similar analysis for many of the OECD countries.[3] The study differed from the first by making adjustments for self-employed, unemployed, and retired union members. In all cases but Britain, the adjusted series shows greater losses in union membership than the unadjusted study did. However, because of the broader coverage of the earlier data, they are preferred here to the BLS series.

There are no similar studies for developing nations. The data for these countries, shown in Table 1.2, were secured primarily from reports by U.S. embassies abroad. They tend to be rough estimates; the best that can be hoped for them is that they are consistent over time.

Table 1.2
Trade Union Density: Developing Countries (Union Membership as a Percentage of the Labor Force)

	Beginning of period	End of period	Percent change over period
Argentina [1]	33[a]	31[b]	- 6.1
Brazil[2]	13.6[k]	12.5[c]	- 8.1
Chile[2]	37[d]	13.2[b]	-64.3
Egypt[2]	27[e]	25[c]	- 7.4
India[3]	30[a]	24[f]	-20.0
Kenya[4]	7.2[k]	4.6[m]	-36.1
Korea[5]	12.8[g]	22[c]	+71.8
Malaysia[5]	10.6[k]	10.1[m]	- 4.7
Mexico[5]	23.4[h]	27.5[m]	+17.5
Philippines[5]	11.4[e]	12[c]	+ 5.0
Taiwan[6]	20.9[k]	30.5[c]	+45.9
Thailand[5]	3.2[k]	2.8[m]	-12.5

Sources: 1. U.S. Department of Labor, *Country Labor Profile* and *Foreign Labor Trends.* "Trade Union membership [in Argentina] increased with the return of democratic government in late 1983 and was boosted in 1989 and 1990 by worker fears over job security in a deepening economic recession." *Foreign Labor Trends: Argentina,* 1990; 2. U.S. Department of Labor, *Foreign Labor Trends* for Brazil, Chile, and Egypt, various issues; 3. U.S. Department of Labor, *Foreign Labor Trends.* The density figures represent the ratio of estimated union membership to the sector of the labor force subject to unionization; 4. U.S. Department of Labor, *Foreign Labor Trends.* There were 650,000 union members claimed in 1980 and 390,000 estimated for 1988; 5. U.S. Department of Labor, *Foreign Labor Trends* for Korea, Mexico, the Philippines, and Thailand, various issues; 6. Republic of China, *Taiwan Statistical Data Book,* 1988, and *Foreign Labor Trends,* Taiwan, various issues; [a]1983; [b]1990; [c]1989; [d]1976; [e]1979; [f]1987; [g]1978; [h]1982; [k]1980; [m]1988.

Note: The inclusiveness of the labor force varies from country to country. Extreme caution should be used in making intercountry comparisons.

A sample of 25 countries has been selected for this book; it includes 13 industrial and 12 developing countries. The former group is composed of the five biggest countries of Western Europe—Britain, France, Italy, Germany, and Spain; the United States and Canada; Australia and New Zealand; Japan; and the three Scandinavian countries. The sample could have been expanded by including all other OECD countries, but they would have added to the burden considerably without much change in the results. With the exceptions of Finland and Ireland, all countries omitted experienced a decline in union density during the 1980s. Non-European countries are included because it seemed preferable to diversify rather than overconcentrate on Europe.

An effort was made to include countries in Africa, Asia, and Latin America to represent the developing group. This proved possible for Asia and Latin America, but African data are scarce. One goal was to include some of the former communist countries, but their labor scene is in such disarray that this was impossible.

Before discussing the data, a few words about their provenance are in order. The term *density* means the ratio of trade union members to the labor force. There are difficulties with both parts of the ratio. Union membership is reported in many different ways. It may include members who are retired or unemployed in addition to those currently at work and sometimes even family members. Regular payment of dues is not always a requisite for inclusion. Where government registration is required, members of organizations that for one reason or another are not required to register are often omitted from official tallies. Sometimes there is a question of whether an organization of employees is or is not a trade union within the meaning of relevant laws.

There are similar difficulties with the concept of *labor force*. It may be defined to include all active participants, including the military, or all nonagricultural participants, or all wage and salary earners—which would exclude employers and the self-employed—or those in the "organizable" or "modern" sector, which would exclude large numbers of "informal" sector workers in developing countries.

The result is that great care must be exercised in making intercountry comparisons. If Country A has a density ratio of 50 percent and Country B 10 percent, it is fair to assume that there is a significant difference between them. Small differences cannot be interpreted in the same way without a careful examination of how the ratios were determined.

Greater confidence can be placed in density time series for individual countries, although even here there may be some problems. Figures for different years are not always derived from the same sources, using a consistent methodology, particularly for developing countries. Caution is necessary where there are big changes in short periods of time. Cataclysmic events—a military coup, for example—can devastate unions, but changes in density tend to be gradual during the normal course of events.

Looking at the data for the countries listed in Table 1.1, the large Australian decline appears to be credible. The Australian Bureau of Statistics put union density at 49.5 percent in 1982 and 40.5 percent in 1990, which is comparable to the decline shown in the table.[4] Canada is an interesting case; while the loss suffered by its unions was small, it was a decline and one that continued afterward.[5]

French union data are notoriously deficient. How many employees actually pay dues to the three major labor federations has long been a matter of speculation. It has been conventional to measure union strength by the votes for candidates put forward by the various unions in elections for factory committees. Whether the decline in French union membership was actually as great as that shown in Table 1.1 is difficult to determine, but a recent study noted, "The official figures are enlightening, but the reality is still more somber. The true problem of France . . . is that it is suffering more from the absence of unions than from deunionization. From the very start, the great mass of employees were cool toward union affiliation, not opposed to the unions but simply outside them. The employees who left the labor movement for the last ten years mainly rejoined the great majority which had never been in them."[6]

The German decline is somewhat surprising in view of the continuing power of its labor federation, but there is nothing to suggest that the figures are inaccurate. The Italian situation is quite different, resembling that of France. The Italian unions tend to include retired and unemployed members in their totals, and membership claims are not firm. There is no reason to doubt the authenticity of the Japanese data, but the decline shown for New Zealand does raise a question. Total union membership fell by 23.5 percent from 1980 to 1990, but whether this covers only the market sector, as shown in Table 1.1, or the entire labor force, is not clear.

As for Spain, an analysis of trade union membership in 1989 concluded, "An accurate estimate of Spain's unionization rate is of course made difficult by the poor state of trade union membership data, but in any case there is no question that it has fallen over the past five years and is one of the lowest in the western industrialized world."[7] The U.S. Embassy in Madrid estimated a density rate of 8 percent in 1989 and noted that "trade unions claim higher affiliation as they include retired workers and whole families."[8]

Little need be said about Britain and the United States in this context. Both countries experienced severe union membership losses during the 1980s. The precise density levels vary with the choice of a denominator for the density ratio.

The Scandinavian countries were included in the sample because of their high density ratios and their resistance to the downward trend in density. There was a small decline in Denmark during the decade, but Sweden and Norway saw growth. There may have been some late attrition. Sweden's large blue-collar union experienced a slight membership loss in 1988 and 1989, but the white-collar and professional federations gained. The U.S. Embassy in Oslo estimated in 1991 that "union membership as a percentage of the total work force has dropped in recent years from about 66 percent in 1958 to its current level of about 60 percent."[9] The latter figure is consistent with the density ratio that appears in Table 1.1. There was a density gain in Norway during the period.

It should be pointed out that the turning points, the years at which union density reached a peak and then began to decline, were not during the 1980s for some countries. For those for which consistent time series are available, French unions reached their high point in 1975, Italy in 1978, Britain in 1979, and the United States in 1953.[10] Still, the 1980s witnessed an almost universal decline.

The data are more problematic for developing nations.[11] The agricultural sector typically employs a large proportion of the labor force, with many of the workers farming on their own. Unionized farm workers are found only where there is a plantation system; Malaysia is an example. Many of the services are low in productivity, petty trades in which most of those engaged are self-employed. Where they exist, unions are rarely well financed, and they are often either adjuncts of a political party or fiefs of ambitious politicians. Unions may simply claim membership on the basis of the support they receive in job actions. There is also a tendency to measure membership against the "organizable" labor force, however that is defined. The best that can be expected is definitional consistency within each country over time.

The density ratios for 12 developing countries are shown in Table 1.2. Argentina has had a well-established labor movement for years. There were 4 million organized workers in 1983, more than one-third of the labor force. Although the unions claimed 4.2 million members in 1990, U.S. Embassy estimates put the figure at 3.8 million, a density of 31 percent. The Brazilian data are less reliable, and the figures that appear in the table must be regarded as rough estimates.

As late as 1976, three years after the Pinochet coup, Chilean trade unions still claimed 1 million members, 37 percent of the labor force and 55 percent of wage and salary earners. However, by 1983 the density ratio had fallen to 16 percent with a further decline to 13.2 percent in 1990. The subsequent fate of Chile's trade unions is discussed later.

Egypt has the largest union membership in the Arab world. There were said to be 2 million members in a nonagricultural labor force of 7.3 million in 1979. Density was reported to be 25 percent in 1989, although the source provides no indication of how this was computed.

The Indian labor force was estimated at 200 to 265 million people in 1979. Claimed union membership in 1980 was roughly 6 million, said to be 25 percent of "the sector of the economy subject to union organization," without any additional specification. It was also noted that "trade union membership claims are not normally accurate reflections of paid-up adherents. Nevertheless, the comparative strength of the various unions is generally considered to be reflected by the membership claims." In 1983, some 30 percent of India's "organizable" sector was estimated to be unionized, falling to 24 percent in 1987. It was noted in 1990 that "whatever growth did occur in trade union ranks generally involved switched allegiances from one competing union to another, with no overall expansion in the number of organized workers in the modern sector."[12]

There is an almost complete lack of trade union data for sub-Saharan Africa. Some countries in the area had labor unions of respectable size at independence, but civil war and coups tended to destroy them. In 1982, for example, the Nigerian Labor Congress claimed a membership of 3 million, 10 percent of the modern work force. There are no subsequent data, but it was reported that 1982 membership "has been drastically reduced by seven years of austerity and high unemployment."[13] The only African country (other than South Africa) for which there are even rough estimates is Kenya, with 390,000 union members both in 1980 and 1988, implying a fall in the density ratio because there was rapid growth in the labor force.

Korea and Taiwan, which have been dubbed NICs (newly industrialized countries), both experienced considerable expansion in density during the 1980s. Korea had 1 million organized workers in 1977, some 12.8 percent of the labor force. By 1989 membership reached 1.83 million for a density ratio of 22 percent. There were 1.1 million unionists in Taiwan in 1980 and 2.23 million in 1988, also yielding a substantial increase in density.

The data for Malaysia are relatively good. There were 524,000 union members in 1980 in a labor force of 4.96 million, a 10.6 percent density ratio. Membership rose to 617,000 in 1988, but the labor force increased slightly more, so that density declined. "After growing steadily up to 1983, trade union membership stagnated from 1983 to 1987. There was a net gain of 10,000 members in 1988. Union membership has failed to match the growth in employment in the 1980s, resulting in a drop in the level of unionization to 10.1 percent in 1988 compared with 11.3 percent in 1985,"[14] the U.S. Department of Labor reported.

The Mexican data must be viewed with caution. The U.S. Embassy in Mexico City reported that there were 9.5 million organized workers in 1989, a density ratio of 25 to 30 percent; the figure shown in Table

2.1 is the midpoint. Estimated union membership in 1982 was 3.4 million in a labor force of 14.7 million, implying an increase in union density between these two years.

The Philippines present a problem. The density ratios were said to be 11.4 percent in 1979 and 12 percent in 1989. A larger increase might have been expected with the overthrow of Marcos, but "union organization in the private sector continued to make modest gains, as it has since the advent of the Aquino administration . . . the laggard area of union organization continues to be in the private construction sector. Less than one percent of construction workers are union members."[15]

Thailand's labor movement was in its infancy in 1979, with only 97,000 members in a labor force of 3.5 million. Unions grew with the expansion of industry, reaching 295,000 in 1988, but government policy had an adverse effect on organization. "Organized labor in Thailand was fragmented and fractionalized even before Government legislation removed State Enterprises from the Labor Relations Act and dissolved unions in this sector in April 1991. Thailand has one of the lowest levels of unionization in the region, with under three percent of the pre-April 1991 industrial workforce organized into unions."[16]

All industrial nations in this sample, with the possible exceptions of Norway and Sweden, witnessed a decline in trade union organization during the 1980s. In 8 of the 13 countries listed in Table 1.1, the decline ran into double digits. This is a remarkable finding when the widely differing conditions facing unions in the countries are taken into account.

The sample of developing countries is limited because of data unavailability, but they tell a different story. Unions in the rapid growers, Korea and Taiwan, unambiguously prospered. They held their own in several other countries but suffered decline, sometimes catastrophic, in a few. There is not the uniformity that characterizes the industrial nations.

Great Britain and the United States were the pioneers in the establishment of trade unions 150 years ago; unions spread to other countries with the growth of industry. The general membership trend was upward, although not always in a monotonic fashion. The union movement throughout the noncommunist world appeared to be in good shape after World War II. Decline set in as early as the 1950s, but it was not until the 1980s that the retreat became widespread. The causal factors are sought in the pages that follow.

ADDENDUM

The data in Tables 1.1 and 1.2 terminate in the late 1980s for the most part. Later statistics are available from another source for some countries. They appear in Tables 1.3 and 1.4 (p. 10).

The data derive from annual reports of United States embassies on

Table 1.3
Trade Union Density: Industrial Countries, After 1988

	Years	Percent change
Australia	1989–1991	– 2.4
Canada	1988–1991	nc
Denmark	1988–1991	nc
France	1990–1991	nc
Germany	1988–1989	nc
Italy	1988–1991	nc
Japan	1988–1990	– 5.4
New Zealand	1989–1991	– 7.0
Norway	1989–1991	+ 5.8
Spain	1988–1991	+ 25.0
Sweden	1989–1990	nc
United Kingdom	1988–1991	– 10.2
United States	1988–1991	– 5.3

Sources: U.S. Department of Labor, *Foreign Labor Trends,* various issues; *Monthly Labor Review,* various issues.
Note: nc indicates no change.

labor conditions in the countries in which they are located. They do not use the same methodology as the OECD data and are not comparable with them. For example, the 1991 embassy density figure for Spain, 10 percent, carries this footnote: "Figures are Embassy's estimate of actual dues paying membership. An OECD report gives a 16 percent figure for 1988 based on nominal membership claimed by trade unions. This figure also includes some family members and retired workers." The embassy estimate for 1988 was 8 percent.

It is probable, however, that the embassy figures are consistent over time, yielding some idea of more recent union membership trends. For the industrial countries, only in Norway and Spain does density appear to have risen between the end of the 1980s and 1991. For the rest, there was either no change or continued decline. Trade unions in Chile, the Philippines, and Taiwan gained considerably during the later period—a not unlikely outcome, at least for Chile and Taiwan—but either decline or no change characterized the experience of the other developing countries.

Table 1.4
Trade Union Density: Developing Countries, After 1988

	Years	Percent change
Argentina	1989-1991	- 7.0
Brazil		na
Chile	1988-1991	+ 47.0
Egypt	1990-1991	nc
India		na
Kenya		na
Korea	1990-1991	- 7.7
Malaysia	1988-1990	- 6.9
Mexico	1988-1991	nc
Philippines	1988-1990	+ 21.0
Taiwan	1988-1991	+ 30.7
Thailand	1988-1991	- 10.7

Source: U.S. Department of Labor, *Foreign Labor Trends,* various issues.
Note: na indicates not available; nc indicates no change.

NOTES

1. Richard Freeman, "Contraction and Expansion," *Journal of Economic Perspectives,* Spring 1988, pp. 69-70.
2. It would have been preferable to cover the entire decade of 1980 to 1990. Unfortunately, the OECD data stop at 1988 and extrapolating the series would have been difficult, if not impossible.
3. Clara Chang and Constance Sorrentino, "Union Membership Statistics in 12 Countries," *Monthly Labor Review,* December 1991, p. 46.
4. Australian Bureau of Statistics, *Trade Union Members in Australia,* Canberra, 1990, Table 1.
5. According to the *Directory of Labor Organizations in Canada,* an official publication, density fell by 1 percent from 1988 to 1990.
6. Michael Noblecourt, *Les Syndicats en Question,* Paris: Les Éditions Ouvrières, 1990, p. 33.
7. Roger C. McElrath, *Trade Unions and the Industrial Relations Climate in Spain,* Philadelphia: Wharton School, 1989, pp. 104-105.
8. U.S. Department of Labor, *Foreign Labor Trends: Spain, 1989-1990,* p. 2.

9. U.S. Department of Labor, *Foreign Labor Trends: Norway, 1989–1991*, p. 3.

10. Jelle Visser, *European Trade Unions in Figures*, Deventer, The Netherlands: Kluwer, 1989.

11. The term *developing* is a misnomer when applied equally to all the countries in this group. Argentina and Chile, for example, have had mature economies for many years. However, because of the nature of their development, they are not members of the OECD and generally are not grouped in the OECD category. They are listed here with the developing countries to simplify exposition.

12. U.S. Department of Labor, *Foreign Labor Trends: India, 1989–1990*, p. 3.

13. U.S. Department of Labor, *Foreign Labor Trends: Nigeria, 1987–1988*, p. 5.

14. U.S. Department of Labor, *Foreign Labor Trends: Malaysia, 1988–1989*, p. 2.

15. U.S. Department of Labor, *Foreign Labor Trends: Philippines, 1989–1990*, p. 9.

16. U.S. Department of Labor, *Foreign Labor Trends: Thailand, 1990–1991*, p. 5.

CHAPTER 2

___

Economic Growth and Industrial Restructuring

Two variables that may be associated with union growth or decline are considered in this chapter. The first is the rate of economic growth, represented by changes in the gross domestic product (GDP). The second is industrial restructuring, the realignment in intersectoral employment shares. The variable selected to represent it is the ratio of manufacturing to total employment.

Economic growth should be a plus for unionization. A growing economy offers more scope than a stagnant one for improving wages and other working conditions. Rising profits may cause employers to look with less disfavor on organization among their employees. With employment opportunities rising, employees are less fearful of losing their jobs if they join unions. With incomes rising, workers are more able to pay adequate dues regularly.

The annual rates of GDP growth for the period of 1980 to 1989 are shown in Table 2.1 for the sample of countries under study. This was not a good decade from an economic point of view. With few exceptions, the GDP rates fell from the levels registered during the previous decade. Trade unions faced a less than favorable economic background during the 1980s..

The question is whether unions in countries with relatively high GDP growth rates experienced lower density declines than those in low-growth countries. Regressions were performed separately for the industrial and developing countries. For the industrial group, there was no significant relationship between the two variables. For devel-

Table 2.1
Average Annual Growth of the Gross Domestic Product, 1980–1989
(Percentages)

Industrial Countries		Developing Countries	
Australia	3.5	Argentina	−0.3
Canada	3.3	Brazil	3.0
Denmark	2.2	Chile	2.7
France	2.1	Egypt	5.4
Germany	1.9	India	5.3
Italy	2.4	Kenya	4.1
Japan	4.0	Korea	9.7
New Zealand	2.2	Malaysia	4.9
Norway	3.6	Mexico	0.7
Spain	3.1	Philippines	0.7
Sweden	1.7	Taiwan	7.2
United Kingdom	2.6	Thailand	7.0
United States	3.3		

Source: World Bank, *World Development Report* (Washington, D.C.: World Bank, 1991); *World Tables,* 1991.

oping countries, however, the correlation coefficient was 0.33 – a borderline level of significance. This suggests that rapid rates of economic growth were of some importance to the new unions in developing countries, and it is evidenced particularly in the data for Korea and Taiwan.

This does not mean that unions do not profit from a growing economy. In all likelihood, they find it easier to maintain their membership and to expand more readily in good times than in bad. However, the GDP growth variable does not appear to be of determining importance for the industrial nations in a comparative international analysis. Other factors may overshadow it.

Restructuring has been a popular explanation of trade union decline. *Restructuring* refers to the migration of production and jobs from such basic industries as steel, automobiles, and appliances, which have been the core of unionization, to the newer high-tech industries and to the service sector. As one writer put it, "Because the U.S. led in structural changes in labor markets, it should and did lead in the decline of private sector unionism, membership, and density."[1] In the case of France, "this loss of membership can be explained by a shift in the pattern of employment. Manufacturing industry has been the traditional heartland of trade union recruitment and France is no exception."[2] For Australia, "since around 1982 . . . structural change has disadvantaged unions, and this accounts for around half the decline in union density since then."[3]

Labor history lends a good deal of plausibility to this argument. In the United States, for example, the great burst of unionization that began in 1935 and raised total union membership from 3.6 million in that year to 14.3 million a decade later took place to a considerable extent in the mass production industries and shifted the balance of union strength from construction, transportation, and coal mining to the manufacturing sector. Thus it is easy to blame the subsequent decline in density on downward employment trends in manufacturing.

Many specific arguments are advanced in support of this interpretation. Those who flocked to the unions in the 1930s were to a considerable extent blue-collar workers who traditionally were easier to organize than white-collar employees. A large proportion of the jobs that opened up in the expanding service sector since the mid-1960s were white collar. Much of the employment in basic manufacturing was originally centered in large factories, which yield a higher return to organizing drives than the more recent smaller working units. The new high-tech industries are capital intensive and require fewer employees. Moreover, many are scattered geographically rather than concentrated in a few states; the geographic concentration of manufacturing jobs characteristic of the United States 60 years ago made it easier to create a political and economic atmosphere favorable to unions than doing so would be today.

Similar explanations have been advanced for other countries. In Spain, "industrial restructuring . . . has struck most heavily where union strength was greatest (steel and engineering, mining, shipbuilding, textiles). Large plants have shed labor or shut down while entire districts . . . have witnessed the disappearance of their principal industries."[4] In Japan, "changes in the employment structure (increased share of workers in the tertiary sector and smaller enterprises), the growth of white collar workers in the occupational structure . . . are among the factors working to depress the unionization rate of labor unions."[5] It should be noted, however, that a number of studies, particularly those of a predominantly econometric character, have concluded that restructuring was not a critical factor in explaining union decline.[6]

To get at the comparative picture, a variable consisting of changes in the ratio of employment in manufacturing to total employment between 1980 and 1989 is used. The argument for using this figure is that

Table 2.2
Employment in Manufacturing as a Percentage of Total Employment

	1980	1989	Percent change.
Industrial Countries			
Australia	22.6	17.8	- 21.2
Canada	21.6	18.5	- 14.4
Denmark	23.2	20.8	- 11.3
France	29.5	23.8	- 19.3
Germany	34.0	31.6	- 7.0
Italy	32.7	27.5	- 15.9
Japan	28.6	27.3	- 4.5
New Zealand	26.7[a]	20.0[a]	- 25.0
Norway	23.1	17.2	- 25.0
Spain	32.9	27.1	- 17.6
Sweden	25.7[a]	23.2[a]	- 9.9
United Kingdom	30.2	28.0	- 7.3
United States	22.4	17.9	- 20.0
Developing Countries			
Argentina	n.a	n.a	n.a
Brazil	16.6[b]	15.7 [c]	- 5.4
Chile	16.1	16.9	+ 5.0
Egypt	n.a	n.a.	n.a.
India	26.3	25.0[d]	- 4.9
Kenya	14.0	13.0	- 7.1
Korea	21.6	27.6	+ 12.2
Malaysia	16.1	15.5[c]	- 3.7
Mexico	12.2	19.2	+ 57.4
Philippines	10.8	10.5	- 2.8
Taiwan	n.a	n.a.	n.a .
Thailand	7.9	9.1[d]	+ 15.2

Sources: 1980: OECD, *Historical Statistics,* 1960–1982; idem, *Trends in Developing Economies,* 1990; 1989: OECD, *Labor Force Statistics,* 1969–1989; ILO, *Yearbook of Labor Statistics,* 1989–1990; *World Labor Report,* 1989.
Note: n.a. indicates not available.
[a]The data for the two years are not strictly comparable; [b]1981; [c]1987; [d]1986.

a relative decline in manufacturing employment should lead to a proportional intercountry loss in density if restructuring is a major explanatory factor. The employment shift could go in one direction only, from manufacturing to services, at least in the industrial nations.

The data for this variable appear in Table 2.2. It is necessary to point out that a declining ratio does not necessarily imply that the absolute level of manufacturing employment has fallen. An unchanged level or even an increase in manufacturing employment would be consistent with a decline in the manufacturing share if service-sector employment were increasing more rapidly. This was the case for Canada and Japan, although most other industrial countries saw a decline in the number of manufacturing jobs.

The data in Table 2.2 were regressed against the union density ratios, separately for the industrial and developing groups. The resultant correlation coefficients were not significant for either group. Employment restructuring measured in this fashion does not account for union density change.

Yet restructuring cannot be dismissed as a contributing cause. Table 2.3 contains membership figures for five major unions in manufacturing and for unions in construction, government, and teaching for the United States and Canada. Except for the Canadian automobile union, there were deep losses in both countries in steel, clothing and textiles, and rubber during the 1980s. The government and teachers' unions increased their membership, while the loss in construction was far less than in manufacturing. The manufacturing unions lost membership largely due to industrial decline occasioned by reduced demand for their products and foreign competition rather than to transformation of employed workers from union to nonunion status.

Norway and Sweden are countries in which an employer threat to the continued existence of unions is unthinkable. Yet the Norwegian Chemical Workers' Union, which organizes workers in aluminum, glass, ceramics, and rubber, lost 9 percent of its members from 1980 to 1990, while the Woodworkers' Union lost 15 percent during the same period. On the other hand, the union catering to employees of local communities had a gain of 38 percent.[7] Membership in the Swedish Metalworkers' Union fell by 2 percent from 1979 to 1991 and rose by 34 percent in the Municipal Workers' Union.[8]

West Germany is an interesting case. Its manufacturing employment share fell by 7 percent and its aggregate union density by 9 percent during the 1980s, yet membership in the giant Metal Workers' Union increased by 2 percent from 1978 to 1989. The country's big gainer was the Public Service and Transport Union, with a 15-percent membership increase.[9] Germany has been undergoing restructuring, but its share of manufacturing employment still remains higher than in the other industrial nations.

18   *Trade Union Growth and Decline*

Table 2.3
Membership of Major Unions in the United States and Canada, 1978 and 1989
(Thousands)

	United States			Canada		
	1978	1989	% change	1978	1989	% change
Automobiles	1420.1	922.0	- 35	133.7	166.6	+ 12
Steel	1097.8	321.0	- 71	202.5	160.0	- 21
Clothing and Textiles	454.4	242.0	- 47	36.1	30.0	- 17
Ladies' Garments	327.1	160.5	-50	21.3	14.5	- 32
Rubber, Linoleum	134.7	86.6	- 36	16.3	13.4	- 18
13 Building Unions	3729.3	2951.6	- 21	368.2	334.9	- 9
State and Local Government	1950.6	2050.0	+ 6	587.3	877.5	+ 49
Teachers	2196.5	2770.0	+ 32	324.6	390.3	+ 20

Source: Pradeep Kumar, *Industrial Relations in Canada and the United States* (Kingston, Ontario, Canada: Queen's University, 1991), 14.

The issue is not whether trade unions in the manufacturing sector of industrial nations have lost members; with few exceptions, they have. The question is why employees in the service sector have not joined unions in sufficient numbers to offset the losses in manufacturing.

As already noted, there appears to be no consistent relationship between changes in manufacturing employment and union density in the developing countries. This was to be expected. Industrialization rather than industrial reconstruction is the current concern of most of these countries. Where there were losses in union density, other factors were at work.

Two countries merit special attention. South Korea and Taiwan underwent rapid industrial growth during the 1970s and 1980s. Manufacturing employment shares have risen in both. Their experience is consistent with what happened in the industrial countries at similar stages of development. Both countries now are shedding the labor-intensive industries on which their initial growth was based and are moving into more capital-intensive industries. Soon their service sectors may begin to invade manufacturing, with a decline in union density possible.

Industrial restructuring was a factor in weakening trade unions in the industrial nations but was neither the dominant nor the major cause. To say, as Freeman does, that "the structural analysis is misleading and should be rejected," is to go too far.[10] But to assert that changes in the structure of industry do have an impact is no explanation. The problem is to determine why unions did not compensate for losses in their manufacturing base by organizing workers in expanding economic sectors.

NOTES

1. Leo Troy, "Is the U.S. Unique in the Decline of Private Sector Unionism?" *Journal of Labor Research*, Spring 1990, p. 115.

2. Jeff Bridgeford, "French Trade Unions: Crisis in the 1980s," *Industrial Relations Journal*, Spring 1990, p. 131.

3. David Peetz, "Declining Union Density," *Journal of Industrial Relations*, June 1990, p. 197.

4. Jordi Estivill and Joseph P. M. de la Hoz, "Transition and Crisis: The Complexity of Spanish Industrial Relations," in Guido Baglioni and Colin Crouch, eds., *European Industrial Relations*, London: Sage, 1990, pp. 286–287.

5. Takeshi Inagami, "The Growth of the Service Economy," *Japan Labor Bulletin*, March 1985.

6. See, for example, Henry S. Farber, "The Decline of Unionization in the United States," *Journal of Labor Economics*, 8(1) 1990, Pt. 2.

7. The data are from Norwegian Federation of Labor, *Temabok*, Oslo, 1991.

8. E. Owen Smith, *Trade Unions in the Developed Economies*, New York: St. Martin's Press, 1981, and U.S. Department of Labor, *Foreign Labor Trends: Sweden, 1991–1992*.

9. U.S. Department of Labor, *Country Labor Profile: Federal Republic of Germany, 1979*, and *Foreign Labor Trends: Federal Republic of Germany, 1990*.

10. Richard B. Freeman, "Contraction and Expansion," *Journal of Economic Perspectives*, Spring 1988, p. 76.

CHAPTER 3

Earnings, Inflation, Unemployment, and Female Employment

This chapter deals with another set of variables that may affect trade union density. The first is the average annual change in manufacturing earnings during the decade. In general, rising wages should favor unions, because they may be attributed to union activity and they facilitate the building of union financial strength. This hypothesis was tested for the United States, with the following result: "Unionism may rise with increases in money wages. Workers apparently interpret aggregate wage increases as evidence of union instrumentality or view unions as a normal good."[1]

Table 3.1 contains data showing the increase in real earnings per employee in manufacturing from 1980 to 1988 for both sets of countries.[2] For neither set is there any significant relationship when regressed against union density. For the developing countries, the result is somewhat surprising. Rapidly rising real wages in Korea and Taiwan were accompanied by high union growth. However, in Mexico, where wages fell during the decade, the unions prospered, which was also true of Thailand. As for the industrial countries, the variance in real wage advances among countries was small, while that for union density was large.

There are some possible explanations for this counterintuitive result. It may be that it is not the average wage increase during a period but rather the timing of increases that impresses workers. A large increase after a successful strike may solidify the loyalty of workers to their union more than steady but moderate increases. Then there is the question of how employees look at the union-nonunion wage differen-

Table 3.1
Rate of Growth of Real Earnings per Employee in Manufacturing, 1980–1988
(Percentage per Annum)

Industrial Countries		Developing Countries	
Australia	0.2	Argentina	1.4
Canada	0.4	Brazil	0.0
Denmark	0.5	Chile	−1.7
France	1.2	Egypt	0.5
Germany	1.7	India	3.4
Italy	0.8	Kenya	−0.1
Japan	1.7	Korea	5.9
New Zealand	−1.0	Malaysia	4.4
Norway	1.7	Mexico	−5.2
Spain	0.8	Philippines	4.0
Sweden	0.6	Taiwan	6.9
United Kingdom	2.8	Thailand	6.3
United States	1.8		

Source: World Bank, *World Development Report* (Washington, D.C.: World Bank, 1991), Table 7.

tial. If it were increasing, unions might be credited with doing a good job, but if it were narrowing, unions might be accused of inactivity. The data necessary to test the latter hypothesis are lacking. For some countries, institutional factors would make such comparisons impossible. In Germany, for example, union wages are automatically extended to all employees in an industry if certain conditions are met. Moreover, where union density is high, there may be no differential because of the effect of the threat of unionization to employers who have managed to remain nonunion. There also may be no differential simply because there is no relevant nonunion sector.

Price inflation might be expected to have an effect on attitudes toward unionism. Everyone is affected, and the results in terms of reduced purchasing power are felt quickly. The reaction of employees is to demand, either individually or collectively, an increase in compensation at least sufficient to maintain their living standards. If their

Table 3.2
Average Annual Rate of Price Inflation, 1980–1989 (Percentage)

Industrial Countries		Developing Countries	
Australia	7.8	Argentina	334.8
Canada	4.6	Brazil	227.8
Denmark	6.0	Chile	20.5
France	6.5	Egypt	11.0
Germany	2.7	India	7.7
Italy	10.3	Kenya	9.0
Japan	1.3	Korea	5.0
New Zealand	11.4	Malaysia	1.5
Norway	5.6	Mexico	72.7
Spain	9.4	Philippines	14.8
Sweden	7.4	Taiwan	2.7
United Kingdom	6.1	Thailand	3.2
United States	4.0		

Source: World Bank, *World Development Report* (Washington, D.C.: World Bank, 1991), Table 1.

unions have succeeded in indexing wages through collective bargaining or political agitation, this would be a big plus for organization. All other things being equal, inflation should provide a favorable milieu for unions.

Average annual rates of inflation for the period of 1980 to 1989 appear in Table 3.2. There are substantial variations in the rates for both the industrial and developing countries, although the Latin American countries are in a class by themselves. However, once more the regressions reveal no significant correlations for either group. Unions did not do well in high inflaters such as Italy and New Zealand or low inflaters such as Japan and the United States. One might have expected Latin American hyperinflation to push employees into collective action, but that was not the case. Nor did the well-behaved price levels in most of the Asian countries appear to have reacted with union density one way or another.

Why is the hypothesis that inflation is propitious for unions not borne out by the data? One answer may be that in most cases, bouts of inflation are irregular in timing, with governments stepping in to stem negative political repercussions through incomes or monetary policies, whereas union organization requires a longer gestation. In Latin America, where inflation has been endemic and continuous, people have learned to adjust through means other than unionization. In these countries, employers do not wait for union demands to make appropriate wage adjustments if they want to keep their workers.

In addition, unions may suffer adverse financial effects from inflation. They live on membership dues, and everywhere there is a great reluctance to support increases. Organizing is expensive, and the erosion of real union income may inhibit their search for new members. In a few countries, union dues are indexed to price changes; these are the lucky ones.

Of the four variables discussed in this chapter, unemployment would appear to be prima facie, the most relevant in explaining changes in union density. Workers often retain their union membership when on temporary leave, but if they are permanently displaced and find employment with a new employer or in a different occupation, they may be lost to the union. The existence of unemployment also has a dampening effect on union organization among employed workers who may be fearful of employer reaction.

Unemployment is often cited as a cause of union decline. According to Waddington, "the evidence suggests that cyclical changes in membership and density are strongly associated with fluctuation in business cycle indicators."[3] In a survey of the literature, Chaison and Rose reported,

It is now widely recognized that labor market conditions have a significant impact on union growth and decline. However, the nature of the relationship depends on how the variables are specified. For example, in Sweden only the level of unemployment was found to be a significant determinant of union growth whereas in Australia the rate of change in unemployment was found to be significant. . . . Bain and Elsheikh found that the rate of change in unemployment exerted the greatest influence in Australia, Great Britain, Canada, Sweden, and the United States.[4]

The variable chosen to test the hypothesis that unemployment is a factor in the determination of union density is the average rate of unemployment experienced by each country during the 1980s. There are no data for 7 of the 12 developing countries in the sample. This is not a serious omission, however. The significance of unemployment in these countries is quite different from what it is in the industrial nations. Unemployment compensation is usually lacking in developing nations, so that people must be doing some work to survive. Their labor markets

Table 3.3
Average Annual Rates of Unemployment, 1980–1989 (Percentage of Labor Force)

Industrial Countries		Developing Countries	
Australia	7.5	Korea	3.8
Canada	7.3	Malaysia	7.4[a]
Denmark	8.9	Philippines	6.6
France	9.0	Taiwan	2.1
Germany	5.9	Thailand	2.8
Italy	9.5		
Japan	2.5		
New Zealand	5.1		
Norway	2.7		
Spain	17.5		
Sweden	2.5		
United Kingdom	10.0		
United States	7.2		

Source: OECD, *Employment Outlook,* July 1991, p. 40; ILO, *Yearbook of Labor Statistics,* 1988, 1989.
[a]1980, 1985–1988

are characterized by large, informal, low-productivity sectors in which hours of work may be long but income is minimal. The problem is underemployment rather than unemployment, and there is no agreed-upon definition for the former. The few figures that are available for unemployment in developing countries are shown with those for the industrial nations in Table 3.3, but their significance is limited.

Unemployment in the industrial nations does appear to be a determining factor when regressed against union density. Twenty-three percent of the variance is explained, with a 6-percent significance limit. Double-digit unemployment was an important factor in curbing union activity, while low unemployment, as in Norway and Sweden, provided a favorable union environment. It should be pointed out, however, that there is still a large area of indeterminacy.

A note about Korea and Taiwan: The stage of development in these

countries suggests that the low rates of unemployment shown for
them in Table 3.3 are meaningful. By 1990, both had exhausted their
supplies of productive labor, and Taiwan was even importing labor.
Their spectacular rates of union growth were undoubtedly influenced
by their labor supply situations. Thailand, however, still had a large
reservoir of labor in its agricultural sector that was readily available
for modern industry and services. Its low reported unemployment level
was essentially meaningless.

The unemployment-density relationship has not been stable over
long periods. For example, the most rapid growth of union membership
in the United States took place during the 1930s, when unemployment
was running in the double digits. German and Japanese membership
shot up in the years immediately after World War II. These increases
were the consequence of unique traumatic events that were not evident
in the industrial nations during the 1980s, when both the political and
economic trends were much smoother. This was not true, however, of
some of the developing countries, when extraordinary events disrupted
normal life.

The final explanatory variable that will be explored in this chapter
involves the rise in female employment. It has been argued that, for
several reasons, women are less prone to unionize than men — less commitment to the labor market, more employed on a part-time basis,
greater representation in the services than in manufacturing. "Arguably
one of the reasons that union density is lower in female-dominated occupations is that unions have historically put less effort into recruiting
and retaining members in those occupations and in part-time employment,"[5] Peetz writes.

Table 3.4 shows the growth rate of female employment as a percentage of total employment during the 1980s, for both industrial and
developing countries. Regressed against union density, there is no significant correlation, although there was a good deal of variance among
countries and female growth rates have been high as women in large
numbers entered the labor force in both sets of countries. It is probably
true that labor unions in most countries have not done all they could to
organize part-time employees or industries with high labor turnover,
for example, but this does not appear to be a significant cause of
declining density on a comparative basis.

Earnings, inflation, unemployment, and relative female employment
were correlated with trade union density on a comparative basis for
the 1980s. The only factor that proved to be significant was unemployment in the industrial countries. These results are not inconsistent
with any strong findings in studies of individual countries over time.
The indication is that we must look for other factors to account for differing rates of intercountry union density change, particularly the
decline that characterized the decade of the 1980s.

Table 3.4
Female Employment as a Percentage of Total Employment in Nonagricultural Activities, 1981-1990 (Percentage Increase, 1981-1990)

Industrial Countries		Developing Countries	
Australia	12.9	Argentina	n.a.
Canada	10.6	Brazil	11.3 (1981-88)
Denmark	0.1	Chile	7.1
France	8.2	Egypt	n.a.
Germany	4.3 (1981-89)	India	15.7 (1981-89)
Italy	8.7	Kenya	14.3
Japan	9.3	Korea	12.5
New Zealand	4.8 (1986-90)	Malaysia	16.1(1981-87)
Norway	9.5	Mexico	4.6
Spain	19.9	Philippines	-0.4
Sweden	3.4	Taiwan	13.6(1981-88)
United Kingdom	10.9	Thailand	7.6(1981-88)
United States	10.7 (1986-90)		

Source: ILO, *Yearbook of Labor Statistics,* 1991.

NOTES

1. Lee P. Stepino and Jack Fiorito, "Toward a Comprehensive Theory of Union Growth and Decline," *Industrial Relations,* Fall 1986, p. 259.
2. It would have been preferable to use earnings for the entire labor force rather than for manufacturing alone, but data for the former are less reliable than for the latter. While the two may diverge over a long period, it is unlikely that they would do so over a decade.
3. Jeremy Waddington, "Trade Union Membership in Britain, 1980-1987," *British Journal of Industrial Relations,* June 1992, p. 306.
4. Gary N. Chaison and Joseph B. Rose, "The Macrodeterminants of Union Growth and Decline," in George Strauss et al., *The State of the Unions* (Madison, Wis.: Industrial Relations Research Association, 1990), pp. 18-19.
5. David Peetz, "Declining Union Density," *Journal of Industrial Relations,* June 1990, p. 197.

CHAPTER 4

The Effect of Government

Government policies can be of critical importance to the survival and growth of trade unions. Despotic national governments do not tolerate free trade unions. A pro-union government can facilitate organization. A government that is more or less neutral can throw its weight on the side of one of the bargaining parties in pursuit of its political and economic goals.

Government influence can be exercised in many ways. Legislation can hinder union operations. Compulsory registration of unions may give government registrars the authority to reject recognition. Particularly in developing countries, many obstacles are often placed in the path of nascent organizations.

Government policy is frequently cited as a factor in the decline of the American labor movement. Employers may use to their advantage laws originally designed to help labor.[1] To quote one study: "For labor organizers and officials, nothing better explained their inability to extend organization than the degeneration of the country's system of labor laws. Ronald Reagan's accession to power in 1981 exacerbated all of labor's problems. Appointment of conservatives to the National Labor Relations Board (NLRB) swung that agency sharply to the right."[2] The AFL-CIO was unrelenting in its criticism of the Bush administration on this count. It castigated the federal government for encouraging the export of American jobs to exploit cheap labor, for imposing delays in the bargaining process, and for condoning the use of permanent replacements to break strikes.[3]

There are problems involved in matching government policy and union fortunes. A classification system is necessary. The extremes are not too difficult, between a social democratic government closely allied with trade unions on the one hand, and an anti-union authoritarian government on the other. It is those in between that are difficult to characterize.

For the purposes of this book, the countries in the sample are classified in five categories. Strongly pro-union governments are rated 5. Authoritarian governments that either ban unions or permit them a limited existence under complete government control are rated 1. A government that is more or less neutral in regard to labor and management is rated 3. Where a government leans toward unions but does not necessarily support them on all matters, the rating is 4. A government that allows unions some degree of independent action but tends to favor employers when disputes arise is rated 2.

The immediate objection that can be raised is that this must necessarily be a subjective process. Equally qualified observers might come up with different scores. But there is no alternative if comparisons are to be made. The best that can be done is to buttress ratings with factual arguments. It should be noted that such a procedure is employed in many other contexts, including the labor market; the determination of wage differentials by job evaluation techniques is a case in point.

A second problem has to do with the consistency of government policy during the 1980s. An election or a coup may change government attitudes toward many things, including unions. Here the countries are classified on the basis of the preponderant policies during the decade and, in close cases, on the situation in the latter part of the decade on the theory that the terminal years better reflect how unions fared in response to traumatic political events.

INDUSTRIAL COUNTRIES

The examination of government labor policies in the industrial countries under review includes categorization of government attitudes toward unionization in each.

Australia

The classification of Australia is a relatively easy task. Beginning in 1983, and for the rest of the decade, the Australian Labor Party (ALP) was in power. Bob Hawke, the country's prime minister, had been president of the Australian Council of Trade Unions (ACTU), the dominant labor federation. A majority of organized workers belonged to unions affiliated with ALP. The constitution of the Western Australian branch of ALP states that "the affiliated unions are an integral part of the ALP and as such shall have the right of direct representation on Elec-

torate Councils, State Executive and State Conferences." Union affiliation fees provided a substantial share of ALP finances. An important
Economic Accord between ACTU and ALP was characterized as follows: "the Accord itself illustrates a special relationship between the
Labor Party and the trade unions. . . . There was no attempt to seek
any such comprehensive agreement with employers, or with any other
section of society."[4]

Although some state governments were less close to the unions, the
general environment was highly favorable for them. Yet density declined by 14 percent during the decade. It is clear that the causes of
union decline in Australia lie elsewhere. Australia belongs in category
5 of the classification scheme.

Canada

Relations between the Canadian labor movement and the national
administration, which was dominated by liberal and conservative political parties, have been described as cool or frosty. The Canadian Labor
Congress (CLC), with about 60 percent of organized workers in its affiliated unions, maintained a consistent opposition to the policies of the
Progressive Conservative government that held office for the latter
part of the decade. The CLC maintained formal ties with the social
democratic New Democratic party, which did manage to capture several provincial governments.

The federal government was not hostile toward unions, which were
invited to participate in a number of government-sponsored institutions. However, the unions opposed several critical government initiatives, including the North American Free Trade Agreement and the
open skies aviation policy. And while Canadian unions have been forced
to make wage and other concessions, this was due primarily to management rather than government pressure. As far as collective bargaining was concerned, the federal government maintained a fairly
even balance between labor and management, in contrast to the situation in the United States. A rating of 3 best characterizes government-
union relationships during the 1980s.

Denmark

Together with Norway and Sweden, Denmark has one of the highest
union density ratios in the world. The Danish labor movement has prospered for more than a century, and it is accepted as a permanent fixture
in the country's institutional structure. Its key role has not been questioned since 1899, when the Confederation of Trade Unions (LO) and
the Danish Employers' Confederation entered into an agreement that

recognized the right of workers to organize and of employers to manage.

The LO enjoys close relationships with the Social Democratic party, which held political power for many years. During this period, the government-union relationship would have merited category 1. During 1982, however, Denmark was governed by a nonsocialist coalition of political parties. However, the tradition of involving the unions in major economic decisions has continued, and there has been no attempt to curb union bargaining power. The well-developed collective bargaining system remained in operation, and the government usually took a neutral position between the bargaining parties. Denmark belongs in category 3.

France

From 1981 to 1992, France was governed by the Socialist party, except for a brief interregnum from 1986 to 1988. This would normally have meant a national administration favorable to the unions, but the structure of the labor movement and its low density complicated matters.

There are three major and several minor union federations split along ideological lines (discussed in more detail in Chapter 5). The largest one, the CGT (General Federation of Labor), was under the control of the Communist party for the entire period under review, and was generally critical of the government. The other two, FO (Workers' Force) and CFDT (Democratic Federation of Labor), maintained closer relationships with the Socialist government, though there was less warmth as the decade went on.

The Socialists enacted legislation that was clearly pro-union, the most important of which was a series of laws passed in 1982, the Auroux reforms, named after the then minister of labor. Their thrust was to make worker representation in an enterprise more effective by requiring annual bargaining between employers and local unions on a wide range of issues. Parties entering into industrywide agreements are to meet annually to negotiate wages.

This and other legislation did not arrest the decline of the French unions, but the government cannot be blamed. Compared with their conservative predecessors, which enhanced union rights only after nationwide general strikes, the Socialists leaned toward the unions but were not absolutely committed or organically bound to them. Category 4 is the appropriate level.

Germany

The German Trade Union Federation (DGB), with more than 80 percent of the country's organized employees, dominates the union scene.

This is in sharp contrast to the situation that prevailed during the Weimar Republic, when the labor movement was split along ideological lines and failed to provide a united front against the Nazis. The men who reestablished the movement after the war were determined to prevent a repetition of this experience.

The DGB is formally neutral politically; it does not support any political party. However, it does maintain closer relations with the Social Democrats than with the Christian Democrats. It was Social Democrats who were responsible for legislation on codetermination, much desired by the unions and opposed by employers.

Since 1982, the Christian Democratic Union has formed the government of Germany in coalition with a smaller allied party. This represents a shift of influence away from the unions. "Between the Social Democratic and the conservative power blocs there exists a fundamental difference in their respective assessments of the market and the role of trade unions. Whereas the former emphasized the inherent imperfections of the market and supported corporatist relations between government and union, the latter blamed excessive union influence for the market's failure to secure prosperity and employment."[5]

Nevertheless, the conservatives have maintained a policy of strict neutrality in industrial relations, largely limiting the role of government to setting the legal framework for collective bargaining. Any other policy would have been counterproductive given the strength of the DGB in the labor market. The rating is a clear 3.

Italy

As in France, the Italian labor movement has been divided along ideological lines. The largest union, at least until very recently, was the General Confederation of Labor (CGIL), dominated by the Communist party but with a socialist minority. Next in size was the Confederation of Workers' Unions (CISL), oriented toward the Christian Democrats, followed by the Socialist Union of Labor (UIL).

Italy has been governed by a fleeting succession of governments best described as center left, with the Christian Democrats the senior partner and the socialists in ascendance on occasion. When it comes to trade union-political relationships,

while the CGIL majority is close to the [Communist party], it is an open question whether the "transmission belt" role of the union for the party is still applicable. The socialist minority of the CGIL, which is automatically granted 30 percent of the confederation's leadership positions, has links with the Italian Socialist Party (PSI). The CISL Confederation is likewise close to the Christian Democratic Party, but it includes socialists and other party followers; however, there are no formally recognized political factions. The UIL has three such factions: Socialist, Republican, and Social Democratic.[6]

A number of former trade union officials sit in Parliament and act as a lobby on matters of interest to labor, giving the unions considerable influence. The government plays an active role, mediating labor disputes of national importance, and while its suggestions may not be to the liking of the bargainers, there is no consistent favoritism to either side. Thus the Italian governments of the 1980s are best described as neutrals, category 3.

Japan

The unique structure of the Japanese labor movement complicates an assessment of its relationship with the government. Briefly, the center of gravity of Japanese unionism lies firmly in the local, or enterprise union, of which there is one for every major firm. Most enterprise unions are affiliated with national industrial unions, which in turn belong to national federations. The national unions and federations are largely coordinating and lobbying bodies.

Until 1989, the federations were split ideologically, but in that year unity was achieved with the formation of a new body, the Japanese Trade Union Confederation (Rengo), the affiliates of which now include about two-thirds of all union members. Before 1989, the largest federation, the General Council of Trade Unions (Sohyo), maintained close working relationships with Japan's largest opposition party, the Socialist party, while the smaller Japanese Confederation of Labor (Domei), was allied with the Democratic Socialist party. These ties might have given the unions a great deal of influence over national policies were it not for one factor: "Since these parties are in the opposition in Japan, and since there has been virtually no prospect of forming a coalition government by themselves in the foreseeable future, the unions have been forced into attempting to influence directly or to apply pressure on the government, or the ruling Liberal-Democrats."[7]

Japan's government has been strongly business oriented, and it might have been expected to lean toward management in the event of industrial conflict. But given the structure of the labor movement, such conflict is almost nonexistent, and preservation of the system is very much in the interest of the government.

There is one sector in which there is direct confrontation between unions and government: the public sector. Public employees do not enjoy the right to strike under Japanese law, a great source of dissatisfaction to them. They have applied to the International Labor Organization for assistance but to no avail. There have been illegal strikes, resulting in the discharge of union officials.

Public service employees are highly organized. In 1990, with a density ratio of 75 percent, they constituted 12 percent of all union members, although their employment share was only 4 percent.[8] Although relations between the unions that represent these employees and the government have been stormy, the unions have not been suppressed. Taken together with the stake of the current government in the continuing prosperity of enterprise unionism, a rating of 3 is appropriate. Any domination of unions comes from employers, not government.

New Zealand

This country was governed by a conservative party from 1975 to 1984. In 1984, the Labor party won a sweeping electoral victory with strong support from the trade unions. It remained in office until October 1990, when it was once more replaced by the National party.

In 1982, the National party government had repealed a law of long standing that permitted the union shop. The result was a precipitous drop in union membership, some unions losing as many as 30 percent of their members. The Labor government restored the union shop in the Labor Relations Act of 1987, together with other rights desired by the unions. But there was one important change from previous legislation: in order to secure the rights, unions were required to register with a government official. In the past, unions with at least 30 members were eligible for registration; the minimum was raised to 1,000 in 1987. The result was many amalgamations and a drastic decline in the number of unions. This also may have had an adverse effect on membership.

Although the Labor government leaned toward the unions in crafting the legislation, its relations with its own employees were poor. As part of a plan adopted in 1984 that was designed to reduce inflation and stimulate economic growth, the government undertook a restructuring of employment in the state sector; as a result, 42,000 employees were laid off during the next five years. Several government-owned enterprises were privatized, over union objections:

National strikes, sectional strikes, deputations, and marshalling of wide support throughout the trade union movement were part of the response of public sector unions. Almost all of the resources of these unions were devoted to this issue in the period November 1987 through April 1988. . . . Consideration of submissions, formal and informal, during the parliamentary process, did achieve changes at the margin and improve the legislative drafting, but the substance and central ideological position of the Government was not altered.[9]

The determination of the Labor government to move the economy toward a greater market orientation was part of a struggle taking place within the Labor party, resulting in reshuffling of the cabinet in 1989 and 1990. The left wing of the party, supported by the trade unions, argued that the economic reform program had weakened the country and almost destroyed the welfare state. Right-wing elements countered by arguing that unless the reforms were effectuated, a welfare state could not be sustained. This internecine struggle reduced the effectiveness of the Labor party and was a major factor in its defeat in 1990.

The conflicting developments make it difficult to characterize the position of government toward unions in the 1980s. The 1987 legislation was clearly pro-union, but as the need to reform the economy grew, the Labor party became more neutral. One way to resolve the dilemma is to compare the Labor attitude with that of the National government that succeeded it in 1990. One of its first acts was to ban the union shop and to deprive the unions of rights that they had long enjoyed. Its stated purpose was to free the labor market from restrictive practices, but the effect was also to weaken the unions, which responded with mass demonstrations. The National government may be fairly characterized as anti-union and, by comparison, the previous Labor government as pro-union. Despite the differences between the two wings of the labor movement, cooperation continued after 1990. The Labor government of the 1980s is in category 4.

Norway

Except for short periods, Norway was governed by the Labor party during the 1980s, supported by small political groups. This continued its domination of the Norwegian political scene for most of the past 50 years.

The Norwegian Federation of Labor (LO), which not too long ago had a virtual monopoly of organized workers, has recently faced increased competition from newer federations. In 1958, LO represented 84.5 percent of all unionized workers, but by 1990 its percentage was down to 60.5 percent, although its membership had grown in absolute terms. Two other groups, the Federation of Norwegian Professional Associations and the Confederation of Vocational Unions, divided most of the remaining unionists between them.

Long before the hegemony of the Labor party, it had enjoyed close relationships with LO and these continue. A book compiled by the Labor party refers to this relationship in the following terms:

When LO was founded in 1899, the trade union and political labor movements were separated. However, the two organizations have a common ideological platform to a considerable degree, and have had different forms of cooperation over time. Today there is only one formal cooperative body, the Cooperation Committee, consisting of representatives of the Labor Party and LO, and usually meeting weekly.... The LO supports the Labor Party economically through donations, among other things for election campaigns.[10]

There has been some criticism of the closeness of this relationship, largely from partisans of a leftist socialist party that caters primarily to professionals and intellectuals. Some voices have been raised in favor of widening LO contacts, but thus far the traditional pattern continues. The other labor federations are not tied to any political party.

The mutual support provided by the political and trade union wings of the labor movement has been successful in raising Norwegian living standards and working conditions to one of the highest levels in the world, and experimentation with new relationships is not likely. The Norwegian trade unions were fortunate in operating in a category 5 milieu during the 1980s.

Spain

The Socialist Worker party has formed the government of Spain since it won a parliamentary majority in 1982. It has followed a moderate economic policy designed to stimulate economic growth, keep inflation in check, and make the labor market more flexible. Some measures that it instituted displeased the trade unions, which felt that the policy of liberalization had gone too far.

The principal ally of the Socialist Worker party is the General Workers Union (UGT), the main competitor of which, the Confederation of Workers Commissions (CCOO), has been under communist influence. Union membership figures are not reliable in Spain, but recent elections for plant-level worker delegates resulted in 42-percent support for UGT slates against 36 percent for the CCOO, the balance going to smaller groups.

The relationship between UGT and the government has been described this way: "Since the restoration of free trade unions, the UGT has relied on the government for a considerable portion of its financing needs, whether in the form of rent-free office space, partial distribution of the 'patrimonio sindical' [funds of the Franco-era unions], or fees for its participation in the government's various institutional bodies."[11] However, unhappiness with government policy of a faction within the UGT led to a one-day general strike in 1989 in support of higher wages and collective bargaining rights for civil servants.

Despite such events, "concrete evidence of the UGT-PSOE [Socialist] relationship is still abundant even though socialist rule since 1982 has placed tremendous pressure on the trade union-party link. For example, PSOE members are required to join the UGT, and in many cases UGT executive committee members also occupy influential positions within the leadership of the PSOE."[12] This might be taken as strong government support for the unions were it not for the existence of the CCOO. The government has been willing to deal with that organization and with UGT on social issues, and it has not placed any obstacles

38 *Trade Union Growth and Decline*

in the way of CCOO, but there is not the same degree of support accorded UGT. Taken together, a rating of 4 best describes the overall government-trade union relationship during the 1980s.

Sweden

Following is a good summary of union-party relationships in Sweden:

The Confederation of Swedish Trade Unions (LO) has long been considered nearly synonymous with the Swedish Social Democratic Party (SDP). For over 90 years, the two organizations have had the same ideology, leadership, and even membership. The two-million plus member LO supplies the SDP with money and ideas, as well as overall organizational support. The SDP considers labor its natural ally and frequently campaigned on the platform that only the SDP can guarantee labor peace.[13]

SDP held political power during the years 1932–1976, either alone or in coalitions. From 1976 to 1982, nonsocialist-party coalitions held a majority, but in 1982 SDP was once more swept into office. In 1991, however, SDP had its worst election since 1928 and became the opposition.

Years of socialist government with close ties to the trade unions would seem to be an ideal setting for trade union prosperity – and it was. Sweden reached the highest level of union density in the world. Sweden owes its organizational preeminence to the fact that almost all white-collar workers and professionals are unionized. But most belong to unions that are not affiliated with the LO. Most white-collar workers are in the Central Organization of Salaried Employees (TCO), while a third body, the Confederation of Professional Unions (SACO), caters to a wide variety of people, most of whom have academic training, including architects, military officers, clergy, scientists, physicians, and dentists. Swedes entering the labor market join unions almost automatically, if only to protect their interests in the competition with other groups for a share of the national product. However, neither TCO nor SACO is tied to a political party.

The unions, including LO and SDP, have differed over economic policy. In 1989, the Socialist government proposed a freeze on wages and prices and a two-year ban on strikes. The legislation was defeated in Parliament, leading to the resignation of the prime minister. He was able to form a new government, but the author of the legislation, the finance minister, was not reappointed. This episode contributed to the socialist electoral defeat in 1991, when 40 percent of blue-collar workers voted nonsocialist.

Whatever the future may hold for the LO-SDP alliance, there is little question that during the 1980s, Sweden had a strongly pro-union government. A majority of TCO and SACO members may have voted against them, but the Swedish socialists were deeply committed to the principle of independent trade unionism and would not have followed a policy that led to union decline in any way. A rating of 5 is appropriate.

United Kingdom

The British trade unions initiated the formation of the British Labour party after the turn of the twentieth century, and a strong alliance has existed between the two ever since. The Trades Union Congress (TUC) and the Labour party are connected organically in that unions enroll their members in the party as a group rather than individually and send delegates to the annual party congress with votes in proportion to their membership. If the union delegates agree on policy, they can control the outcome of resolutions that come before the congress. It has been established, however, that Labour members of Parliament are not bound by congress resolutions.

From 1945 to 1979, there were alternating Labour and Conservative governments. The Conservatives, while not strongly hostile to the unions, were more inclined to back employers. When Labour was in office, the unions enjoyed strong support from the government. In general, all the governments of this period maintained good relations with the unions on matters of social policy.

All this changed abruptly in 1979 with a Conservative victory at the polls. Prime Minister Thatcher did not conceal her hostility toward the unions and whittled down their power by legislation:

The range and number of contacts between ministers and union leaders, which had grown steadily since 1940, declined immediately the Conservative government took office. The government has also announced that unions would henceforth no longer be regarded as a major interest meriting representation on public bodies considering matters of general importance; their advice would be sought solely on questions directly affecting the work interests of parts of the labor force.[14]

Several studies placed a large part of the blame for the decline of the British unions squarely at the door of the Thatcher regime.[15]

There is no doubt that the unions faced a hostile political environment during the 1980s. It is tempting to attribute their heavy membership losses to this factor alone. However, other forces were at work, and given a more favorable economic situation, they might have been able to do better. As for the rating of the government attitude, a level of 2 seems appropriate.

United States

Until the advent of the New Deal and the Franklin D. Roosevelt administrations, U.S. labor maintained a policy of neutrality between the two major political parties – the Democrats and the Republicans. In every presidential election since, with one exception when it remained neutral, organized labor has backed the Democratic party. Several Republican administrations subsequently were more or less neutral between labor and management, but this came to an end in 1981 with the Reagan and Bush administrations.

President Reagan signaled his intentions during the famous strike of air traffic controllers, when all the strikers were discharged and replaced at first with military and then with newly trained civilian personnel. The close ties that had existed between the unions and the Labor Department, which administers a number of programs of importance to the unions, were broken with the appointment of secretaries of Labor with little experience or sympathies for the unions. Decisions of the National Labor Relations Board, which is charged with policing labor relations, became increasingly pro-employer as conservatives came to dominate it. Legal firms specializing in advising employers how to prevent unionization proliferated.

It has been argued that union decline had begun well before the 1980s and continued during the Democratic administration of President Carter. All that happened during the 1980s, the argument continues, was a redressing of the previous tilt of federal policy toward the unions. This point might refute an assertion that union decline was primarily a result of government policy, but it does not address the question of government attitudes.

One would have to go back to the 1920s to find federal administrations that were less inclined than the Reagan and Bush administrations to regard trade unions as legitimate and important institutions in the political and economic life of the country. It may be that this development can be ascribed to the theory that union practices were increasingly hampering American employers in competing with Japan and Germany for markets. Whatever the reasons, when viewed against the broad sweep of American labor history, the federal administrations of the 1980s belong in category 2.

DEVELOPING COUNTRIES

Some developing countries have long but not very successful histories of industrial development, while others have become full-fledged industrial nations in recent years. None is a member of the rich nations' club, the OECD. None is classified as a "high-income" economy by the

World Bank. Only Brazil and Korea were listed by the Bank among the "upper-middle-income" countries on the basis of 1989 per capita income, although Taiwan would be in this category if it were recognized as an independent nation. Despite great differences in their economic and social backgrounds, it is convenient to treat these countries as a single group for the purposes of this study. However, there is much greater variance in labor market conditions among them than among the industrial nations, and this extends to trade unionism as well.

Argentina

This has long been a puzzling country for economists. At the turn of the century, its gross national product was not much different from that of Australia. In 1989, the ratio of its per capita GNP to that of Australia was only 15 percent. Argentina was the most rapidly growing country in Latin America in the early part of this century, but it has practically stopped growing for the past 50 years. It has great national resources and has benefited from heavy European immigration. Yet it has a long history of economic mismanagement, including periods of hyperinflation that stifled economic progress.

Argentina's labor movement has had a long and checkered career. During World War II, it fell under the influence of Juan Perón and has remained faithful to his corporatist doctrines ever since. "Organized labor is basically led by union officials with close allegiance to the Peronist movement, although not all union leaders are Peronists. This ideological brotherhood, however, has not kept the union movement from splitting over personal or sectoral differences."[16] As long as Perón or his followers held political power, the unions occupied a favored position. When Perón's opponents came into office, the unions suffered along with the Peronists.

There was a vivid example of this in 1976, when a military junta took over the government. One of its first acts was to suspend most trade union activities. The right to strike was abolished, union leaders were kidnapped and murdered, and the assets of the dominant General Confederation of Labor (CGT) were seized. Union power was seriously eroded.

Table 1.2 shows that the initial year for the determination of change in Argentina's union density was 1983, the year in which constitutional government was restored and the labor movement could begin to function freely. The assets of the CGT were returned, but the process of rebuilding was slow, hampered by the opposition of the unions to the economic policies of the Alfonsin administration. It took four years before the precoup situation was reestablished. In 1989, the Peronist party led by Carlos Saul Menem won the presidential election and took over the reins of government, but by then the decade was almost over.

Determining the political atmosphere that prevailed during the 1980s is complicated by the government shifts that took place during the decade. The initial years were characterized by government oppression, followed by six years of a more or less neutral administration.

The behaviour of the past suggests that key elements of a divided Argentine union movement will continue to fight hard to maintain labor's traditionally strong autonomy from state control, an autonomy that has survived repeated efforts at cooptation or repression, and one which seems quite exceptional in the Latin American context. Argentine labor leaders . . . are aware that a strong state has historically been evanescent; labor quiescence or pacts with the government have been traditional short-term survival tactics prior to the reemergence of a renewed labor-based Peronism facing a once again divided state.[17]

Category 3 would seem appropriate.

Brazil

Until 1985, Brazilian trade unions were subject to restrictive laws that had been enacted in the late 1930s by the government of Getulio Vargas, which was modeled on Italian fascism. Despite subsequent modifications, the basic structure persisted. The state was to serve as an intermediary between labor and management. Conflicts of interest were to be resolved by special labor courts. Union structure was dictated by the government; there was no single labor federation but rather independent industrial federations. The principal function of the unions was to administer social welfare programs. Strikes were forbidden. Unions were financed by a tax of one day's pay per annum for each worker.

The system began to fall apart even before 1985, when a civilian regime replaced a government that, like all its predecessors since 1964, had been headed by retired generals. During the late 1970s, there were many strikes, culminating in large mass demonstrations designed to legitimize growing independent unions. A New Trade Union movement was formed in opposition to the official unions despite severe government repression. Nineteen top leaders were arrested and charged with the crime of organizing an illegal strike.

After much internal strife within the nascent labor movement, the Central Union of Workers (CUT) was founded in 1983. However, a dissenting group that favored less militant confrontation with the government established a loose rival federation, which eventually became a full-fledged second central body in 1986 under the name of General Workers Central (CGT).

CGT favored negotiation with the government to achieve modifications of the labor code and defended continuation of the annual day's tax as a means of ensuring adequate financing. CUT insisted on complete independence of government and the right of workers freely to organize as they choose, but CGT feared that this would open the way to fragmentation. CUT had ties to the Workers party, the Democratic Labor party, and a variety of Trotskyist groups and dissenting communists. CGT was allied with the two main communist parties and a number of centrist political groups. A third union central, the Independent Labor Union (USI), was also created in 1986, dominated by the leaders of the old official unions.

All the unions were active in the presidential campaign of 1989, but they were divided in their support. CUT backed the Workers party, but CGT came out for Fernando Collor de Mello, a political novice who was the eventual victor and who was eventually removed from his post in 1992 for alleged corruption.

By the late 1980s, the unions were mostly freed of the shackles that had been imposed upon them by the corporate state half a century earlier: "By 1984, the growth and mobilizational power of the New Union Movement forced the recognition of organized workers as a major political actor. No longer was it possible for the state to simply repress the movement in order to silence the demands of workers."[18] The national administrations that governed from 1985 to 1990 were absorbed in efforts to reduce inflation and bring about economic stablilization, often against union opposition when wage control was at issue. Restrictive legislation remained on the books, but union strategy was simply to disregard it, and the government did not attempt to enforce limitations on union activity, including strikes. On the other hand, it was not government policy to encourage union growth. A classification of category 3 is in order, particularly for the latter part of the decade.

Chile

The Chilean labor movement is one of the oldest in Latin America. In 1976, union density reached 37 percent, but the impact of the Pinochet coup was to put it on a downward slide: "At the beginning of the military regime, the *Central Unica de Trabajadores* was dissolved by decree, as occurred de facto with other important federations; together with the death, imprisonment, and exile of many leaders, these factors tended to paralyze union activities. The regime prohibited collective bargaining and elections, union meetings were subject to extreme control."[19]

A so-called Labor Plan was enacted to weaken the unions that managed to survive. Among other things, it banned union security clauses;

only single-enterprise units were permitted to engage in collective bargaining; contract provisions concerning the size of work crews, the tempo of production, promotion systems, and the use of machinery were banned. Disputes of national interest were made subject to compulsory arbitration. The right to strike was suspended from 1974 to 1979 but was restored in 1979 with some limitations: They could not last more than 60 days and an absolute majority of the employees involved would have to agree to stop work. Temporary replacements could be hired during the 60-day period, but thereafter the strikers were assumed to have resigned their jobs.

A new labor code was enacted in 1987 by the Pinochet government. It improved the situation of the unions but still restricted freedom of association and collective bargaining. Things changed only when the democratically elected Aylwin government was inaugurated in 1990. New legislation removed restrictions on strikes and permitted industrywide bargaining. During 1990 alone, union density rose from 10 to 13 percent.

Groups of unions managed to maintain some cohesion under Pinochet although there were no legally constituted national centers. As a result of looser control late in the decade, Chile had three federations. The largest was the Unified Workers Control, which played a leading role in opposing Pinochet rule. The Democratic Workers Central split into two factions in 1990. A third federation, the Chilean Workers Central, was founded in 1989 by several unions, the leaders of which had been charged with cooperation with the Pinochet regime.

Although unions were allowed to function on a limited basis during the Pinochet period, their ability to represent their members was severely circumscribed. The military regime scarcely regarded trade unions as legitimate social institutions. However, they did permit them to exist and, during the latter part of the decade, to operate more freely. For this reason, Chile is in category 2 rather than 1, which is reserved for complete suppression.

Egypt

The 1980s were uneventful for the Egyptian labor movement. A pioneer in Arab unionism, the Egyptian Trade Union Federation (ETUF) enjoys a monopoly. There were no ideological divisions in the labor movement. However, the unions are surrounded by government regulation and cannot operate freely.

There are 23 national unions, based primarily on separate industries, all required to affiliate with ETUF. Most employees are in the public sector; a large proportion of the remainder is in the informal sector. Strikes are forbidden by law, and collective bargaining is permitted only in the private sector and then only on nonwage issues. Labor disputes are resolved by the courts. In return, public employees enjoy permanent employment, while private employees can be discharged only after lengthy proceedings.

There have been occasional strikes but to lead one is dangerous because of a law stipulating life terms at hard labor for strikers who threaten the national economy. The courts have tended to be lenient in enforcing the law, but the government has overruled them on occasion.

Until recently, it was the practice of the head of ETUF to hold simultaneously the position of minister of Manpower and Vocational Training in the government. Now the minister is chosen from among the presidents of the constituent national unions. This creates a close relationship between government and unions.

The Egyptian government is in some ways a beneficent employer operating is a sea of underemployment. Opposition to its control over unions is lessened because almost 2.5 million Egyptians, 17 percent of the total labor force, are working abroad in other Arab countries. The overall situation is difficult to characterize: The lack of union independence might suggest a rating of 2, but on the other hand the unions do provide some protection to their members and private employers are not given free rein to set labor conditions. A ranking somewhere between 2 and 3 would seem appropriate, but because some degree of internal democracy prevails within the unions, a rank of 3 is justified.

India

The government of India and its constituent states are heavily involved in labor relations. If contract disputes cannot be settled directly by the parties, the first step involving the government is conciliation. Although the conciliator is supposed to end the intervention in 14 days, this is rarely done. Conciliation proceedings can last for months, during which strikes or lockouts are illegal. However, this ban is frequently violated because the government has no effective means of enforcement.

If agreement is not reached during the conciliation period, the matter is submitted to the Ministry of Labor or its state equivalents. Should the parties not agree to voluntary arbitration, the ministry has the power to refer the matter to a labor court for final adjudication. Whether to refer is entirely within the discretion of the ministry. This gives weak unions a way out. In arbitration, what counts is legalism rather than union power. This system enables unions to achieve gains out of proportion to their strength.[20]

The arrangement confers on government authorities a great deal of power over industrial relations. They can bolster weak unions by referral or constrain strong ones by letting them fight it out with the employer. Given that employers are under no legal obligation to recognize a union and that unions are generally weak, particularly in a situation of endemic unemployment, the continued survival of the union movement suggests that it has enjoyed government support. This conclusion is fortified by the fact that India's largest labor federation, the National Trade Union Congress, has had traditional ties with the Congress party, which has been in power for most of the period since India gained its independence. Political parties rely heavily on union support, and when they attain office they can reward the unions for their electoral contributions.[21] This amounts to a rating of 4.

Kenya

The modern system of industrial relations in Kenya goes back to pre-independence days and was eventually embodied in the Industrial Relations Charter of 1962, which provided for union recognition, freedom of association, and peaceful settlement of labor disputes. However, the Ministry of Labor eventually dominated labor relations. Unions were required to register in order to engage in collective bargaining. They had to win representation elections in order to be certified. All new agreements required approval by an industrial court to be valid.

Wages and conditions of labor for specific trades, industries, and occupations are fixed by tripartite industry wage councils. Unresolved disputes may be referred to a board of inquiry or to the industrial court for settlement. The minister of labor may prohibit a work stoppage if the minister feels that there is a possibility of reaching agreement by further negotiation.

The unions are substantially under control of the government, which permits them to function under severe restraints. Union leaders profess their loyalty to President Moi and promise not to call strikes, which are usually led by shop stewards when they do occur. There is always the threat of deregistration, and occasionally this takes place when there is union recalcitrance, as in the case of the Timber and Furniture Workers Union in 1988. As Kenya drifted toward political autocracy and brought all the country's institutions under government control, the trade unions, which had played a significant role in the struggle for national independence, also found their freedom of action curtailed. A rating of 2 seems appropriate.

Korea

The Korean labor movement has historically been heavily controlled by the government. This was particularly true under the Fifth Republic of President Chun Doo Hwan (1980–1987). The situation changed drastically after ruling party presidential candidate (and subsequently President) Roh Tae Woo promised democratic reform in an historic speech on June 29, 1987. Since that time the labor movement has grown in terms of size, diversity, and independence. Nevertheless, the union movement today is heavily divided, and remains limited by a labor relations structure that puts emphasis on enterprise unions, while limiting the roles of regional and functional union bodies.[22]

The effect of the change in regime was dramatic. The union density ratio was 15.5 percent in 1986 and 22 percent in 1989, an increase of 42 percent over the three years. Inevitably, labor conflict escalated.

The Chun government had enacted legislation that severely limited the ability of unions to organize and bargain collectively. Bargaining was permitted only at the enterprise level, and the enterprise unions were forbidden to accept advice or assistance from higher union echelons. Although employer unfair labor practices were forbidden by law, there was little in the way of enforcement. The Federation of Korean Trade Unions (FKTU) had been established under the administration of Park Chung-hee and, although there was a good deal of repression, managed to achieve a membership of 1.1 million by 1980. Under Chun, this dropped to 775,000 by 1987.

A series of amendments to the labor law was enacted in 1987 and the years that followed. Among other things, they abolished the power of the government to dissolve unions and loosened restrictions on strikes and collective bargaining. One consequence was a wave of strikes, often tinged with violence. Another result of the new industrial scene was the splintering of the labor movement. In opposition to the FKTU, so-called democratic unions were formed and refused to join the FKTU on the grounds that it had cooperated with the Chun government. They eventually set up a rival federation, the National Council of Labor Unions.

While the Roh government was much kinder to the unions than its predecessors had been, it could by no means be called pro-union. For example, when the national council was formed, many of its leaders were jailed for violating a law forbidding establishment of more than one union at each level of organization. The government barred the formation of a teachers' union on the grounds that unions were not allowed in the public sector. When it came to ordinary labor disputes, however, although the government often intervened in the interest of wage and price stabilization, it did not usually come down in favor of employers. A rating of 3 is appropriate for the post–1987 Korean government.

Malaysia

This country has a well-established system of industrial relations. This is not to say that there is a completely free labor market. The government has retained supervision of the conduct of collective bargaining, and the power of the unions was kept within strict bounds. Laws enacted in 1977, 1980, and 1988 set the framework for bargaining and gave the government authority to intervene in disruptive strikes.

Enterprise-level unionism is the normal, although not mandatory. The government may invoke compulsory arbitration and prohibit such union demands as clauses covering promotion, transfer, hiring, and dismissal when dealing with so-called pioneer firms for a period of five years in order to encourage investment in new enterprises.

The dominant labor federation is the Malaysian Trade Union Congress (MTUC). The largest union is the National Union of Plantation Workers, which has achieved a high degree of organization on the large rubber plantations. But "the government, particularly the Prime Minister, sees in-house unions as creating a better industrial relations climate between employers and workers, in part because one union would represent all workers in a firm. The leaders of the national unions see them as weakening their own unions and reducing the protection union membership affords a worker."[23]

Despite the degree of government control, the Malaysian system is by no means authoritarian. The unions have defended the interests of their members in a number of areas of employment. Strikes are permitted, and unions do engage in political action. MTUC officers have run for Parliament under the banner of opposition parties. Category 3 is the appropriate rating.

Mexico

The relationships between government and trade unions in Mexico are unique and difficult for an outsider to appraise. Since 1929, the Institutional Revolutionary Party (PRI) has dominated Mexican politics. It has elected every president and most state and congressional candidates during that period. No other Latin American country can begin to match Mexico for political stability.

Until 1991, the membership of the PRI was made up of three major groups: labor, popular, and farmer. Labor was represented by the Confederation of Mexican Workers (CTM), which claims to have 60 percent of all organized workers in its affiliates. Its secretary general, Fidel Velazquez, has held that post continuously since 1950. The CTM is closely integrated into the government structure:

It interacts with business and with government officials to discuss labor demands. The active presence of many public officials at labor congresses and, reciprocally, the presence of the CTM secretary general at many government functions, illustrates the close relationship that exists among these actors. . . .

The presence of federal deputies in Parliament recruited from the labor sector and their increasing relative weight among the PRI delegation is one indication of the importance of labor representation in the governing coalition.[24]

So-called independent unions are joined with the CTM in an umbrella organization, the Labor Congress, which presents to the government labor positions that are outside the bounds of CTM jurisdiction. This is a loose organization and is not part of the PRI. There are a number of independent federations, the largest of which is that of government employees.

Collective bargaining is well established, although government wage guidelines are treated with respect by the unions, particularly the CTM. The government has been careful, for its part, to prevent any undermining of the official leadership by demanding untenable concessions. Wage limitations are compensated by food subsidies and fringe benefits. It is all carefully orchestrated within the PRI structure.

The right to strike is guaranteed by the constitution and by the Federal Labor Act. Unions must first file notice of intent to strike with the employer and the state conciliation board and only after having received the approval of two-thirds of the workers involved. Strikers are entitled to partial or full wages from the employer during the strike. In the event of an illegal strike, an employer may hire strikebreakers and discharge the strikers.

All this suggests that Mexican unions operate within a favorable environment, but there are qualifications. It is not clear how much influence the CTM exercises within the PRI and government decision-making bodies. In all probability, it fluctuates from time to time, depending on economic pressures. The PRI began to change its structure after the 1988 general elections, in the course of which labor's representation on key policy bodies was reduced. A direct challenge to government authority by even an important labor leader can bring swift retaliation and removal of the offending official. Independent unions in the automobile, aviation, and metalworking industries have on occasion sought wage increases beyond the government guidelines but were careful to follow all legal requirements and have refrained from any threats to the political system.

Mexico's labor movement enjoys a protected status as part of the country's basic political and economic structure. No other Latin American labor movement occupies so favorable a position. However, it does not have full equality with the political forces that it supports but occupies a subordinate position in the hierarchy. In this sense, Mexico falls below the European countries in which the trade unions can and do differentiate themselves from closely allied political parties when there are policy differences. The appropriate ranking is 4.

The Philippines

The Philippine labor scene underwent an abrupt change when Ferdinand Marcos was retired in 1986 and was succeeded by Corazon Aquino. Earlier, the labor movement had enjoyed relative freedom from government control for many years, but its effectiveness was limited by fragmentation into competing groups. When Marcos declared martial law in 1972, legislation was enacted that allowed unions to continue their activities only on a limited basis. The 1974 Labor Code guaranteed the right to organize, but it prohibited strikes in "vital" industries, which pretty well blanketed the economy. Most disputes were settled by compulsory arbitration.

The election of Aquino occasioned a wave of strikes as the bonds were loosened. A new constitution that came into effect in 1989 provided the framework for an orderly system of industrial relations. Intervention in the collective bargaining process by the Labor Ministry was limited to disputes that involved enterprises "indispensable" to the national interest.

Unfortunately for the labor movement, much of the new freedom of action went into intense interunion rivalry. A new federation, the May First Movement (KMU), arose to challenge the traditional Trade Union Congress (TUCP), accusing the latter of undue cooperation with the Marcos administration. TUCP espouses cooperation with employers; KMU calls for militant action to raise class consciousness. Much trade union membership resides in unaffiliated local unions, many led by ambitious politicians. The bargaining power of the Philippine unions is low. The expectation that the Aquino administration would further their cause failed to materialize but neither did it seek to hinder their growth or reduce their independence. In fact, the labor relations legislation of 1989 was sponsored by Sen. Ernesto Herrera, who was secretary general of TUCP. Category 3 best describes the attitude of government toward the unions during the latter part of the 1980s.

Taiwan

Until 1987, Taiwan was under martial law. The Chinese Federation of Labor, the only central body in the country, remained in existence but was subject to severe restrictions. Its affiliated unions were forbidden to call strikes or to bargain over wages. Half the officers were members of the Kuomintang, until recently the only legal political party in the country. Collective agreements with employers were reached on a variety of issues, excluding compensation. Despite the handicaps, union membership rose from 765,000 in 1975 to 1.87 million in 1987.

A major change took place in 1987 with the introduction of limited political democracy, and by 1989 union membership was up to 2.53 million. Strikes were legalized, but a string of defeats led to a loss of union momentum. The government was slow in reforming a restrictive labor code that had been enacted in 1975.

During the strike wave of 1988 and 1989, the tendency of the government was to back the tough anti-union stand adopted by many employers, although it did not actually ban the strikes. Up to 1987, the government was clearly hostile to the idea of independent unions, fearing that they might secure wage increases detrimental to economic growth. The attitude of the government eased after 1987 but not sufficiently to make the government a true neutral between labor and management. The desire of Taiwan's workers to organize is indicated by the growth of union membership to 2.7 million in 1990. This marked a new phase in the country's system of labor relations, but the decade ended without the passage of any legislation guaranteeing union independence. For the decade as a whole, the appropriate rating is 2.

Thailand

As in the case of Taiwan, the chief problem faced by the Thai unions was lack of political democracy. The country was governed by a succession of military men with an occasional interregnum of elected officials. In 1980, Field Marshal Prem Tinsulanan assumed the post of prime minister and remained in office until 1988. In that year, General Chatichai Choonhavan became the first popularly elected prime minister in many years and was somewhat friendly to the unions. He was ousted in a military coup in 1991.

The Thai unions benefited because the generals who took over in 1976 were not as repressive as their predecessors had been. Membership rose from 50,000 in 1975 to 217,000 in 1983 and grew further to 309,000 by 1989. The latter figure, however, represented a density rate of less than 3 percent, giving Thailand one of the lowest rates of union organization in south Asia. To make matters worse, the labor movement was split into five rival centers and even these were riven by internal factionalism.

The public sector of Thailand is a large employer, and half of all union membership consists of public employees. To illustrate the attitude of the military toward unions, one of the first acts of the military junta in 1991 was to remove state employees from the jurisdiction of the Labor Act of 1975, which had been installed by a democratically elected administration and guaranteed some union rights. All existing state enterprise unions were dissolved, and employees were permitted to set up "associations" if 30 percent of the employees of an individual enterprise signed a petition in favor. The new associations were forbidden to call strikes and were not permitted to federate with private-sector unions.

It is clear that during most of the 1980s, Thai unions faced an unfriendly national regime. After a promising start during the last few years of the decade, a repressive curtain came down. However, the fact that unions continued to exist and operate suggests that the appropriate rating is 2.

SUMMARY

What can be read from these observations? The data in Table 4.1 show the country ratings established in this chapter. When compared with the trade union density changes during the 1980s that appear in Tables 1.1 and 1.2, only at the extremes does there appear to be any relationship between the two variables for the industrial nations. The three countries in category 2 suffered fairly heavy membership losses, while Norway and Sweden, rated 5, were the only two with gains. There was a membership loss in Australia despite the favorable rating. There was also a wide range of membership loss among countries rated 3. Perhaps the most surprising finding was that three countries in cate-

Table 4.1
Government Attitudes Toward Trade Unions (Ratings 1 to 5)

Industrial Countries		Developing Countries	
Australia	5	Argentina	3
Canada	3	Brazil	3
Denmark	3	Chile	2
France	4	Egypt	3
Germany	3	India	4
Italy	3	Kenya	2
Japan	3	Korea	3
New Zealand	4	Malaysia	3
Norway	5	Mexico	4
Spain	4	Philippines	3
Sweden	5	Taiwan	2
United Kingdom	2	Thailand	2
United States	2		

Code:
 1. Unions banned or under complete government control
 2. Employers favored by government
 3. Government neutral between labor and management
 4. Unions favored by government
 5. Government strongly pro-union

gory 4 – France, New Zealand, and Spain – experienced substantial membership declines.

The picture is somewhat more consistent for the developing countries. The greatest membership loss was sustained in Chile, while the Mexican unions clearly profited from their favorable status. Unions in low category countries, Kenya and Thailand, did relatively poorly. The two outlyers are Korea and Taiwan, where membership increase was far out of proportion to government attitudes. In any event, a regression of the government attitude variable against changes in union density does not reveal any significant correlation between them, for either the industrial or developing countries.

CONCLUSIONS

In the industrial nations, neutrality tends to be the modal government attitude. Unions have a long history, and while the government in office may favor one or the other side of the bargaining table, it is not likely to take an extreme position or seriously damage the labor movement.

The role of government is more important in developing countries, where unions are more fragile and tend to be pawns in political struggles. Authoritarian governments can and do virtually destroy trade unionism, as occurred in Chile.

Some striking exceptions are worthy of further exploration. Severe membership declines in France, Spain, and New Zealand appear to have little relationship to the attitudes of their governments. In Korea and Taiwan, unions achieved tremendous gains in short periods of time with little more than the tolerance of their governments.

The overall conclusion is that at the margin, government attitudes toward unions may be useful indicators of union viability. In general, however, the indicator does not work well in explaining changes in union density.

NOTES

1. Michael Goldfield, *The Decline of Organized Labor in the United States* (Chicago: University of Chicago Press, 1987), p. 225.

2. Robert H. Zieger, *American Workers, American Unions, 1920–1985* (Baltimore: Johns Hopkins University Press, 1986), pp. 195–196.

3. See, for example, *AFL-CIO News*, April 13, 1992.

4. D. W. Rawson, *Unions and Unionists in Australia* (Sydney: Allen & Unwin, 1985), p. 71.

5. Otto Jacobi and Walther Muller-Jentsch, "West Germany," in Guido Baglioni and Colin Crouch, eds., *European Industrial Relations* (London: Sage, 1990), p. 131.

54 _Trade Union Growth and Decline_

6. U.S. Department of Labor, _Foreign Labor Trends: Italy, 1989-1990,_ p. 12.

7. Tashio Shirai, _Contemporary Industrial Relations in Japan_ (Madison: University of Wisconsin Press, 1983), p. 338.

8. Estimated from data in Japan Institute of Labor, _Japanese Working Life in Profile_ (Tokyo: Japanese Institute of Labor, 1991-92), pp. 14, 49.

9. _The New Zealand System of Industrial Relations_ (Wellington: Industrial Relations Center, 1989), p. 108.

10. Norwegian Federation of Labor, _Temabok_ (Oslo: Norwegian Federation of Labor, 1991), p. 49.

11. Roger C. McElrath, _Trade Unions and the Industrial Relations Climate in Spain_ (Philadelphia: Wharton School, 1989), p. 108.

12. McElrath, _Trade Unions,_ p. 111.

13. U.S. Department of Labor, _Foreign Labor Trends: Sweden, 1989-1990,_ p. 4.

14. Colin Crouch, "The United Kingdom," in Baglioni and Crouch, eds., _European Industrial Relations,_ p. 332.

15. See Richard Freeman and Jeffrey Pelletier, "The Impact of Industrial Relations Legislation on British Union Density," _British Journal of Industrial Relations,_ July 1990, p. 142; Brian Towers, "Running the Gauntlet: British Unions under Thatcher, 1979-1988," _Industrial and Labor Relations Review,_ January 1989, p. 163.

16. U.S. Department of Labor, _Foreign Labor Trends: Argentina, 1990,_ p. 6.

17. Edward C. Epstein, _Labor Autonomy and the State in Latin America_ (Boston: Unwin Hyman, 1989), p. 32.

18. Epstein, _Labor Autonomy,_ p. 63.

19. Epstein, _Labor Autonomy,_ p. 83.

20. E. A. Ramaswamy, _Power and Justice_ (Delhi: Oxford University Press, 1984), p. 6.

21. E. A. Ramaswamy and Uma Ramaswamy, _Industry and Labor_ (Delhi: Oxford University Press, 1981), p. 203.

22. U.S. Department of Labor, _Foreign Labor Trends: Korea, 1990-1991,_ p. 3.

23. U.S. Department of Labor, _Foreign Labor Trends: Malaysia, 1990-1991,_ p. 11.

24. Epstein, _Labor Autonomy,_ p. 180.

CHAPTER 5

The Quality of Trade Union Services

A number of trade union attributes help determine the effectiveness with which the unions can pursue their goals. One of the most important is their unity. A united labor movement that does not have to devote time and resources to fending off the raids of rival organizations can devote itself to advancing the interests of its members without diversions. Separate groups of workers cannot be played off one against the other by an employer. The union can speak with one voice before legislative and other government bodies. It can concentrate its political efforts on a single party.

Most labor movements around the world are fragmented. Ideological and religious differences are among the most common but not the only reasons for the fragmentation. Unions sponsor or are sponsored by political parties, mostly on the left. Nonpolitical unions exist but they are scarce. International labor federations – the International Confederation of Free Trade Unions, the World Federation of Trade Unions, the World Confederation of Labor – provide financial and other assistance to national bodies that are in accord with their ideological views.

Division in labor movements is also based on other factors. White-collar workers, professionals, and public-sector workers are often represented by unions organized independent of the traditional blue-collar unions. Highly skilled workers may prefer unions that cater to them exclusively. Trade unions, like other social institutions, tend to be conservative when it comes to structural change. Consolidation does occur, but it often entails years of preliminary negotiation.

Another factor relevant to the quality of a union's services is the effectiveness with which its representation functions. Does it engage in untrammeled collective bargaining with employers? What is the scope of bargaining—the enterprise, the industry, the entire labor force? Does it handle employee grievances and with what success? Does it enjoy the right to strike if negotiations do not result in agreement?

A union's independence of government or employer domination is still another factor in assessing its effectiveness. There are many shades of influence, and it is often not easy to evaluate them. Are enterprise unions that are oriented primarily toward cooperation with their immediate employers rather than with other unions in the same trade or industry genuinely independent? In the past, class consciousness helped prevent such alienation, but it has been fading away with the changing structure of employment.

The financial resources available to unions are also important. Are the funds in the union treasury sufficient to support full-time professional officers? Does the money come from membership dues or from governments or employers? This is a difficult problem for unions in developing countries, where members cannot afford even minimal dues. In industrial countries, members are often loathe to vote an increase in dues in the face of rising prices.

Freedom from corruption is another important factor in union quality. Union history is replete with examples of embezzling treasurers and officers who use their positions for personal gain. Syndicalist unions tried to guard against this possibility by limiting officers' salaries to the maximum wage paid in their trade. Many socialist labor movements looked askance at union salaries that provided a standard of living higher than that of an ordinary working person.

The first to organize were blue-collar workers, and only much more recently have white-collar and professional employees formed unions. With the decline of manufacturing and the growth of the service sector, the power of a labor movement can depend critically on its ability to attract these people. The failure to do so can leave unions stranded with a diminishing portion of the labor force.

The purpose of this chapter is to determine whether the quality of union services, as defined here, is related to their growth or decline during the 1980s. To make intercountry comparisons, an exercise similar to that in the previous chapter is required. It is open to the same objections: There is no way to make evaluations completely objective; the results are influenced by the biases of the evaluator; the weights accorded the various components are not scientifically determinable; the relevant factors themselves may change over time.

Why not use an objective index such as wage gains to measure union effectiveness? Can union-nonunion wage differentials in similar occupations or industries be used as an index of union quality? Much work has been done in the United States in an attempt to isolate the union effect in this manner.[1] There are several difficulties with this approach in making international comparisons, however. Other things are rarely equal among countries of different sizes and with widely varying economic structures. Then there is the practical consideration that non-union sectors with which to make comparisons may not exist. In Germany, for example, union wage scales may be extended by law to an entire industry, regardless of the membership situation, under appropriate circumstances.

For this analysis, the trade union movement in each country in the sample is given a rating of from 1 to 5. A rating of 1 means that the movement barely functions and perhaps exists only because the government wants to impress foreign countries with its adherence to human rights. A rating of 5 is accorded a labor movement that is highly endowed with all or most of the favorable factors cited. A rating of 4 means that unions are quite effective but lacking in some important respect. A rating of 2 is superior to 1 in that the unions, although relatively weak, are more than a showpiece and have some real authority in the labor market. A 3 rating indicates that the labor movement is able to represent the interests of its members with some success but is flawed in other respects.

It might be possible to devise a system that would assign points for specific union characteristics along the lines of job evaluation techniques. In the final analysis, however, the manner in which points are allocated and totaled would be open to the same objections as those that can be raised against the looser evaluation process adopted here. For example, a labor movement might be allotted 5 points for its unity but no points at all because of its complete domination by government. Simple averaging would yield 2.5 points, which would suggest that the union was doing a creditable job in representing its constituents. The informal system adopted here would yield a conclusion nearer the truth.

AUSTRALIA

At first blush, the Australian labor movement appears to have an ideal structure.

In one sense, Australian unionism has become remarkably unified. . . . With only a handful of exceptions all Australian unions of any importance belong to the ACTU (Australian Council of Trade Unions) or, at least, to one of the State Trade and Labor Councils, which are branches of the ACTU. . . . There never was a time when there were rival union federations, divided along lines of politics or religion, comparable to those which have been common in Western Europe. . . . Australia has one of the world's most unified trade union movements.[2]

However, there is a considerable diffusion of membership along with unity at the top. There were 295 separate unions in 1990, 146 of which were affiliated with ACTU. Many of them are small; 188, each with fewer than 3,000 members, accounted for only 3.9 percent of total union membership. On the other hand, the 12 largest, each with more than 80,000 members, had 43.5 percent. In order to have access to important government tribunals, unions are required to register with federal or state registrars. After 1993, federal registration requires a minimum of 10,000 members, although smaller unions can continue to register at the state level.

Most Australian unions are based on occupation rather than industry, accounting for the continued existence of small organizations. Others are limited to employees of a single institution or enterprise, and many are confined to one state. Industrial unions are rare, and one of the results is that many employers must deal with a variety of unions. This would seem to be a recipe for disaster, both in terms of collective bargaining practices and union power. How can small unions secure the resources necessary to function efficiently?

The ACTU has been urging mergers, but many small unions continue to operate successfully. There are several reasons. Small size may be a source of strength rather than weakness if the union involved occupies a strategic niche in an industry. An example is the union of airline flight crews, which has been able to mount crippling strikes. Another reason is that once a union is registered, it enjoys some legal protection against raids and has the exclusive right to represent its members before government tribunals. However, the size limitation that goes into effect after 1993 will make it difficult to establish new unions based on craft or occupation.

The public sector is well organized with a density of 67 percent against 31 percent for the private sector. Women have been a major source of membership growth since the 1960s, but they still lag behind men. In 1990, 35 percent of women were organized, compared with 45 percent of men.

An aspect of Australian industrial relations that would appear to limit union effectiveness is the absence of a legal right to strike. All disputes that cannot be resolved directly by the parties must be submitted to federal or state industrial relations commissions for final adjudication. Australia is unique among industrial nations in its longstanding requirement of compulsory arbitration.

Again, there are mitigating factors. While unions can be fined for engaging in work stoppages, there has been no serious effort to enforce penalties for two decades. They are liable for damage suits by employers, but very few have been successful. "Australia has had a wide experience of laws against strikes, and of difficulties in their application.

It would be hard to argue that anti-strike laws have had more than a marginal or temporary effect in preventing and limiting industrial disputes."[3]

Although the closed shop is not legal, so-called preference clauses in arbitration awards serve the same purpose. When people are being hired, preference must be given to specified individuals, usually but not exclusively union members. Many employers prefer to hire union members in order not to complicate an already-tangled representation situation. Thus, what appear to be serious obstacles to the efficient operation of Australian unions melt away when the system of industrial relations is taken into account. Australian trade unions have been major social institutions since the beginning of the twentieth century and are appropriately rated 5.

CANADA

The Canadian labor movement is not as unified as that of Australia. The dominant central body is the Canadian Labor Congress (CLC), which has almost 60 percent of the country's organized workers within its ranks. A rival body, the Canadian Federation of Labor (CFL), was founded in 1982 by unions in the building trades that opposed the policies of CLC, particularly its political support of the socialist New Democratic party. A third central body, the Confederation of National Trade Unions (CNTU), is confined almost entirely to Quebec and has supported the independence movement in that province. Each of the two latter organizations represents about 5 percent of organized workers. There are also several smaller federations.

The most recent source of union membership growth in Canada has been the public sector. By 1980, almost all eligible public employees were organized, including white-collar employees and professionals. Women are also fairly well organized: 30 percent in 1987 compared with 40 percent of men.

The potential for interfederation strife has been minimized, because CFL and CNTU have been confined to construction and Quebec, respectively. However, jurisdictional disputes have plagued CLC. CLC tightened its antiraiding regulations in 1988, although workers can still change unions if they can show that their current union is not doing an adequate job.

Collective bargaining is decentralized, and the most common bargaining unit is the single enterprise. CLC does not engage in bargaining, nor does it control the policies of its affiliates. A bone of contention during the last two decades arose because many Canadian local unions were affiliated with national unions in the United States (explaining the term *international union* as used in the United States) and were thus subject to outside control. The problem was largely resolved by the secession of many Canadian locals from their U.S. parents and the granting of greater autonomy to those that continued their affiliation.

The Canadian unions have been well financed, but there have been some recent strains. "Never has there been such a great demand for more sophisticated union services and a decreased capacity to pay for them. In particular, structural changes in the labor market have resulted in reduced real dues income per member as overall income has remained stable with new members either working part time or earning less in the general service occupations."[4]

The close alliance between CLC and the New Democratic party is hardly a plus for the labor movement. Although the party has had some success at the provincial level, it has had far from a majority at the federal level, with little chance of coming into power. There are proponents of apolitical unionism in Canada and not only in CFL, but the prevailing ideology of CLC means it is likely to continue the course it followed during the 1980s.

The Canadian labor movement falls short of the Australian on several counts. It is divided at the top, and its political stance has led to cool relations with the government in power and to isolation from consultation on national economic policy. "Labor leaders believe that none of the provincial or federal governments have really accepted the institution of collective bargaining or unionism. . . . Labor leaders have become more skeptical of governments in recent years because of the public policy initiatives on free trade, privatization, and deregulation, and the 'anti-labor' legislative thrust in a number of jurisdictions."[5] The appropriate numerical rating is 4.

DENMARK

It is not difficult to determine a rating for the Danish labor movement. The Danish Trade Union Federation (LO) was founded more than a century ago. Its legitimacy and independence have never been challenged. It is well financed by dues and by ancillary commercial operations that cater to working people. More than half of all organized workers are in unions affiliated with LO. The only other federation of any size is the Federation of Civil Servants and Salaried Employees, with a membership in 1989 about one-quarter that of LO.

The structure of LO differs greatly from union federations in most other countries. The early unions catered primarily to craftspeople and were not disposed to admit the semiskilled. The latter organized themselves into the General Workers Union, stretching across many industries in manufacturing, transportation, construction, and agriculture. A majority of the 31 national unions affiliated with LO are still craft oriented, some of them quite small—photographers, hairdressers, and lithographers, to name a few. The two largest unions, the General Workers and the Shop and Office Workers, have 45 percent of total LO membership between them.

Employers are also well organized in the Danish Employers' Confederation (DA), with which 52 employer associations are affiliated. Collective bargaining is carried on directly between LO and DA on matters of general importance—hours of work, for example—and between national unions and employer associations on issues involving individual industries and trades. Bargaining is highly stylized through long years of experience, and while it occasionally breaks down and is followed by work stoppages, these are unusual departures from the norm.

About 30 percent of all employees are in the public sector and are 90-percent organized. Women constitute 47 percent of the labor force and 48 percent of trade union members. There is a separate LO Union of Women Workers with almost 100,000 members, mainly semiskilled, paralleling the largely male General Workers. The high degree of organization of white-collar and female employees is one of the distinctive features of Danish trade unionism, accounting for its 73-percent density rate.

LO has had close ties with the Social Democratic party, which was in the parliamentary opposition until recently. This has not been a handicap for LO, because the socialists constitute a large parliamentary bloc. Moreover, the unions are the largest interest group in Denmark and must be consulted on economic and social policy. There is no question that the effectiveness of the Danish unions and the quality of their services entitle them to a rating of 5.

FRANCE

Copenhagen is a short air flight from Paris, but moving from the Danish labor scene to that of France is to enter a different world. French trade unions have never gained recognition as permanent fixtures in the social landscape. They are disliked by employers as well as by many potential members. They are among the weakest unions in the industrial nations.

This is not the place to detail the long and checkered career of the French labor movement. Suffice it to say that almost from the start, it has been beset by internal ideological struggle. The French trace their revolutionary tradition to 1789, but it does not include the concept of stable trade unionism.

The labor market institutions that were in place during the 1980s typify much that went before. There were three major union federations: the Democratic Confederation of Labor (CFDT), the General

Confederation of Labor (CGT), and the Workers' Force (FO). CFDT originated as a split from a confessional (Roman Catholic) organization and gradually evolved into a socialist body espousing worker self-management. CGT, after many years of strife, came under the control of the Communist party and remains there. FO was founded in 1947 as a reaction to communism and professes a mild social democratic orientation. Among the smaller independent federations are the Confederation of Christian Workers, the General Confederation of Cadres (which includes engineers, salespeople, and supervisors), and the National Federation of Education.

As already noted, French trade union membership data are unreliable, because there is no tradition of regular dues payment. The relative strength of the various federations is customarily measured by the votes their slates receive in biennial elections to plant-level works councils, which are mandated by law for every enterprise with more than 50 employees. On the basis of 1990 results, CGT received 25 percent of the votes, CFDT 21 percent, and FO 13 percent. Nonunion slates garnered more than any of the federations, 26.6 percent. Estimates of union membership as a whole in 1989 are on the order of 2 million, down from 3.4 million a decade earlier. By way of comparison, there were 2 million trade union members in Denmark in a labor force of 2.8 million, while the French labor force numbered more than 25 million.

While the figures may give the impression of complete impotence, French unions are not without influence. Until early in the 1980s, most collective bargaining was on an industry basis, but legislation enacted in 1982, the so-called Auroux reforms, stimulated enterprise-level bargaining. Employees were given the right to be consulted on the content and conditions of work, the authority of the works councils was enlarged, and annual negotiation of wages, hours, and rationalization was made obligatory. Thus the unions could exercise some authority directly and some through their members on works councils.

Other aspects of the legislation also were designed to bolster union power. All employees may benefit from the terms of a collective agreement whether they are union members or not. Multiple unionism prevails in many enterprises, and if the unions do not present a common front, a collective agreement is valid even if only one union has signed it. However, a nonsignatory union can veto an agreement if it contains certain clauses, provided it is backed by a majority of the works council. Checks and balances make collective bargaining feasible, even in an intensely competitive situation.

The works councils also contribute to the viability of the bargaining system. They and so-called elected employee delegates handle individual grievances. The works councils have advisory authority on some issues and the right of co-decision on changes in profit-sharing arrangements and working hours, among other things. These plant-level bodies help make up for the absence of a unified union presence, although unions can also set up locals and appoint shop stewards.

One principal means by which unions exercise power is the strike. Strikes tend to be short and disruptive rather than drawn-out tests of strength. The public sector is particularly strike prone. Among those engaged in work stoppages in 1989 were railway workers, tax collectors, prison guards, and hospital interns. One reason for the short length of strikes is that unions cannot afford strike benefits. On the other hand, replacements for striking workers are rarely available, so all work stops. To emphasize their seriousness, workers may occupy their plants.

What this adds up to is that French unions, despite their low membership, their fragmented structure, and their poor financial situation, are able to exercise a fair degree of bargaining power through government support and because the revolutionary tradition of French workers makes them willing to heed strike calls. They play a more important role than their density would seem to imply. A rating of 3 seems appropriate.

GERMANY

As already noted, the German trade union world is dominated by the German Trade Union Federation (DGB), which represented 86 percent of all organized workers in 1990. Apart from the DGB, there were three smaller groups: the Confederation of Civil Service Officials, the Salaried Employees Union, and the Christian Trade Union Confederation. When the German labor movement was reorganized after World War II, strict industrial unionism was adopted in place of the prewar crafts. There are 16 national industrial unions in the DGB, ranging in 1991 from the giant Metalworkers Union (IG Metall) with 3.3 million members to the Leather Workers with 72,000.

A brief reference to the German codetermination system is essential to an understanding of the country's industrial relations structure. It was introduced by federal legislation first enacted in 1951 and amended several times thereafter. In its present form, it operates on a two-tier level. Works councils must be established in every enterprise with at least five employees if the employees so desire. Elections for council membership are held every three years, and lists of candidates may be proposed by unions or nonunion groups of employees. Eighty to 90 percent of those elected are usually union members, giving unions substantial control of the councils.

Works councils are not formal union bodies, but they do replace local unions. They enjoy a good deal of authority, including the right to co-determine with employers working-hour arrangements, leave scheduling, health and safety measures, and social services but not wage levels. They must be consulted on scaling down or closing a plant, changes in organization and equipment, and the introduction of new technology. They may not call strikes; all differences with management on matters subject to codetermination are submitted to tripartite arbitration boards.

At the corporate level, firms with more than 2,000 employees are required to include on their supervisory boards (equivalent to boards of directors in the United States) a number of employee members equal to those elected by stockholders. At first glance, this might appear to be representational parity for the employees, but this is not the case. Senior executives and salaried employees are entitled to representation in proportion to their numbers, and they may be expected to vote with management. Moreover, in the event of a tie vote, the board chairperson, who is elected by a two-thirds majority of the board or by the stockholders, casts the deciding vote. The unions have attempted to secure true parity but have not been able to do so.

Employee members of the board have the same authority as those elected by stockholders. They participate in all major decisions, including selection of top managers, and they have access to the books and records of the enterprise. The employee members usually include the chairperson of the works council, one or more officers of the national union, and technical experts nominated by the union.

A question arises about the role of employee directors in collective bargaining. The nature of the bargaining process lessens the possibility of conflicts of interest. Most bargaining takes place on a national or regional level between national unions and employer associations. Collective agreements tend to be multi-employer in scope. If bargaining takes place at the enterprise level, employee board members generally abstain from participation.

German trade unions thus have great influence over business policy at both the corporate and shop levels. They are well governed and generously financed. Yet union density fell during the 1980s. Among the reasons that have been cited are high unemployment; the relative growth of groups that are less prone to organize, including white-collar workers and engineers; management efforts to imbue employees with a greater degree of loyalty to the company; and a Conservative party federal administration.[6] To this might be added the failure of the unions to address the special problems of women. For example, the Public Service Workers Union sought to discourage part-time employment but finally recognized that this ran counter to women's desires.

Overall, the density rate was 47 percent for men and 22 percent for women in 1986.

Whatever their limitations, it would be difficult to fault the German labor unions on structure, bargaining power, or internal management. They occupy a central and stable position in working life and are among the most effective unions in the world. Their rating is clearly 5.

ITALY

There are some resemblances between the labor movements in Italy and France. Both are fragmented along political lines, they have limited financial resources, and they have suffered substantial losses in density. However, the Italian unions tend to be better organized and to play a more extensive and formalized role in collective bargaining.

There are three major labor federations: the Italian Confederation of Labor Unions (CISL), which claimed 2.2 million active members in 1990; the Italian Union of Labor (UIL), with 1.2 million active members; and the General Confederation of Labor (CGIL), with 2.7 million active members. CISL was oriented toward the Christian Democratic party, UIL toward the Socialists, and CGIL toward the Communist party, at least until 1991. There are also several smaller federations.

Factory councils consisting of union shop stewards were formed in the 1970s and were recognized as the union presence on the shop floor. An echelon of informal bodies has emerged recently, so-called base committees, composed of members of all the federations, and are designed to unite skilled professionals who believe that their interests are not being adequately represented. They have been particularly successful among railroad engineers, airline employees, and school teachers.

The national union affiliates of the federations bargain at both industry and plant levels, while the federations bargain on issues of national importance. The government intervenes frequently and on occasion enacts into law matters in dispute that could not be agreed upon by the bargaining parties. National labor contracts are negotiated every three years and apply to all workers in the sectors covered by the agreements. These are supplemented by company-level contracts.

The unions have almost continuously been engaged in tripartite discussions with government and employer representatives in efforts to control inflation and stimulate economic growth. The many federal administrations that have come and gone have been well aware that anything to do with the limitation of labor costs, employment, and welfare expenditures require prior discussion with the unions.

Strikes are fairly frequent, and as in France, mostly take the form of brief demonstrations. The unions enjoy the dues checkoff, and employees may devote 10 hours a year to union business. However, their access to company information is limited. Because of their ties to political parties, their organizational strength in the public sector is 54 percent, well above their overall density.

Despite disunity at the top, the Italian unions have considerable power in labor market questions. If they should eventually merge into one federation, a prospect that has improved with the demise of communism, they would constitute a formidable force. As it is, however, their effectiveness is best characterized by a rating of 3.

JAPAN

Until 1989, there were two major and several minor labor federations in Japan. The largest was the General Council of Trade Unions (Sohyo), with 3.9 million members in 1989. Next was the Japanese Confederation of Labor (Domei), which had 2.2 million. The Federation of Independent Unions (Churitsuroren) had 1.56 million members. Sohyo was an active supporter of the Japanese Socialist party, the nation's main opposition party; Domei was allied with a smaller party, the Democratic Socialists, while Churitsuroren was neutral politically.

In 1989, after years of negotiation, the Japanese labor movement finally achieved near unity. A new organization, the Japanese Trade Union Confederation (Rengo), formed by a merger of the previous federations, emerged with a membership of 7.6 million (1990). Remaining outside were two smaller bodies, one of which was sympathetic to the Communist party. In addition, 3.9 million workers were in unions not affiliated with any federation, so that there was a grand total of 12.3 million union members.

Rengo has some 75 national union affiliates, which in turn are composed of unions limited to a single enterprise. What makes Japanese union structure different from those in all other industrial nations is that the locus of money and power is at the enterprise union level. Federations are primarily lobbying organizations, while the national unions as a group do engage in bargaining with all unionized employers once a year in what is known as the Spring Offensive. However, the enterprise unions are essentially autonomous, and they can follow or reject national union recommendations depending on what they perceive to be the interests of their companies. The larger Japanese firms, almost all of which are unionized, follow the practice of commitment to lifetime employment for their regular employees, hired directly out of school. Once hired, a male employee can expect to remain with the firm until retirement, the average age for which is 60. Women and temporary employees who are hired from the labor market do not enjoy tenure.

This makes for a special relationship between a firm and its regular employees. A Japanese scholar described it in the following terms:

Japanese unionists are really hesitant to cause any severe damage to the enterprise to which they belong. This is not because of their submissiveness to their employer or to management, but because of their identification with, or a sense of belonging to the enterprise to which they belong. If a worker serves a particular enterprise for many years during which he has good prospects for improving his wages, skills, position and status, it is quite understandable that he would acquire an interest in and concern about the enterprise; thus both employer and employee come to share a common desire to maintain the enterprise and to keep it prospering as much as possible. The enterprise becomes a kind of community to which employees tend to commit themselves.[7]

During the Spring Offensive, the entire union movement formulates wage demands to which employers respond. The settlement is generally along the lines of the employers' counteroffer. What is usually a wage increase is based on a combination of changes in the cost of living and productivity. In addition, each firm normally pays its employees a bonus twice a year; the amount depends on its performance.

There are no works councils. A good deal of consultation takes place; at the corporate level, management and enterprise union officials meet several times a year to discuss reports on company progress and future plans. Production committees meet monthly to discuss production schedules. Among the issues taken up in joint consultation are prospective changes in job content, working hours and vacations, health and safety measures, and welfare benefits.

The role of employee participants in the various consultation committees is to receive information and suggest improvements. They have no power to make decisions, and they can neither delay nor veto management initiatives. In theory, the enterprise unions handle grievances, but even when a formal grievance mechanism is contained in a firm's collective agreement with the union, it is rarely invoked. Grievances are said to be adjusted through informal discussion, but there are no data on outcomes.

Enterprise unions receive subsidies from employers in the form of office space, secretarial services, and the like. The officers of these unions are often drawn from lower management levels and are not career unionists. Most expect to advance in the management hierarchy and even some day to be elevated to the boards of directors. Many officials of national unions retain their original company identities and expect to return to the companies when their terms of union service expire.

Strikes are rare in Japan. It is customary for the railway unions or some other public service organizations to close down their enterprises for a day or two during the Spring Offensive negotiations to emphasize the serious nature of the union demands. But it has been 30 years since a major Japanese firm has been shut down by a strike of any duration. The firms can count on fulfilling their work schedules uninterrupted by labor controversies.

The trade union structure leads to a kind of union elitism. Only a portion of the labor force of a large firm consists of workers with job tenure. Many others are hired on a temporary basis or are employed by contractors who work exclusively for one company. They are not eligible to join the enterprise union. The same applies to most women, who normally leave their jobs with the big firms in their mid-twenties. Their density ratio was 18.9 percent in 1990, compared with 29.9 percent for men. Many women work in industries such as textiles that employ mostly women or for smaller firms that are not unionized.

A key question in evaluating the Japanese enterprise unions is whether they are dominated by the employers. Most Japanese insist they are not, that the prevailing structure is a logical response of working people to the permanent employment commitment. Would it make sense for workers to do anything that might reduce the profitability of the enterprises in which they expect to spend their entire working lives?

The other side is that many employer practices, including employer subsidies and the election of management officials to union office, would be considered evidence of company domination in most countries. The complete absence of strikes is an index of union docility. The economic results of union activity also point to a lack of effectiveness. Japan is a wealthy country; its per capita GNP in 1989 was $23,800 U.S. dollars, compared with $20,900 for the United States and $20,400 for Germany. Yet hourly wages of Japanese manufacturing production workers was only 1,478 yen against 1,589 for the United States and 1,799 for Germany. In 1991, Japanese workers were still on a 46-hour week, and many had not yet achieved a five-day week, although shorter hours has been one of the principal union demands. The Japanese Ministry of Labor reported that annual working hours per person were 2,076 in 1989, higher than in any of the industrialized democracies. Part of the reason is the custom of performing voluntary uncompensated overtime as well as the failure of employees to take more than 60 percent of legally due vacations.[8] The explanation that is usually given for this failure is peer pressure, the fear of being regarded as soldiering on the job (i.e., not working at full capacity) when the company needs extra services, although employer intimidation is also cited as a contributing cause.

It seems logical that really effective trade unions would have secured shorter working hours and, in all probability, higher pay some years ago. Their failure to do so is not a reflection of their unwillingness to demand both but a sign of weakness. Labor's alliance with the perennial minority Socialists has contributed to lack of power at the macro-economic level. A rating of 3 for Japan's unions might be considered generous by some. Japanese experts may object, but they should compare the status of their unions with those of countries such as Germany and Sweden before being too critical.

NEW ZEALAND

Although there is only one national trade union federation in New Zealand, the labor movement is not truly united. The New Zealand Council of Trade Unions (NZCTU) was formed in 1987 by a merger of two federations, one in the private and the other in the public sector. About one-half of all unions and three-quarters of union members are affiliated with it. Outside and generally in opposition to NZCTU are a number of loosely coordinated, more conservative unions. The differences are largely ideological. The first president of NZCTU was also head of the small communist-oriented Socialist Unity party, and the federation generally took a left-wing position in the internecine warfare that wrecked the Labor government during the later years of the decade.

When the Labor party came into power in 1984, it was committed to a return to free wage bargaining in place of the previous system of compulsory arbitration, similar to the Australian system, and to the restoration of the union shop. Both were soon achieved. During the 1980s, unions that registered with the government enjoyed considerable protection. They had the exclusive right to bargain for all employees within their jurisdictions. Anyone working under a union shop agreement was required to join the union on pain of discharge. A registered union could seek to extend its jurisdiction, but if another union objected, the issue was settled by a ballot of the workers involved. However, unions could be sued for strikes in violation of contract, a provision aimed at wildcat strikes.

Some provisions were modified by the National party government that came into office in 1991. Registered unions were deprived of the inherent right to represent particular groups of workers. The union shop was abolished and monopoly union jurisdiction dropped. However, these changes were not retroactive and did not affect the situation that prevailed during the 1980s, when the unions were fully protected.

In determining a rating for the New Zealand labor movement, the legal environment under which they were operating must be taken into account. They were rewarded for their close relationship with the Labor party. Before 1984, they lost some members because of the absence of the union shop, but they had the opportunity to recoup during the latter part of the decade. The split in the political regime during the decade and internal union divisions lead to the conclusion that their position was not as strong as in Australia and that a rating of 4 rather than 5 is appropriate.

NORWAY

The Norwegian Federation of Labor (LO) has been the country's dominant union for almost a century. Consisting of 28 national unions, it had a membership of 786,000 in 1990. The only other national bodies were the Confederation of Vocational Unions (YS), with 182,000 members, and the Confederation of Professional Associations (AF), with 208,000 members. YS and AF are oriented toward white-collar and professional service employees, although LO also has membership among white-collar employees in government and commercial activities.

Norway's density is not as great as in Denmark and Sweden, where there was almost 100-percent organization in manufacturing, compared with 87 percent in Norway. There were similar disparities in construction, trade and transport, and in community and social services. The relatively small size of many Norwegian enterprises may account for some differences.

LO has increased its membership in recent years but not as rapidly as the other federations. This has been particularly true in such expanding sectors as health, education, finance, and commerce. In 1962, about 14 percent of all wage earners were employed in these sectors, rising to one-third in 1990. By that time, 21 percent of the sector's employees were in LO unions and 51 percent in the other federations. Some members of LO were not enthusiastic about organizing these people, lest it change the traditional blue-collar character of the movement and the close alliance between LO and the Labor party. The other federations are politically neutral, an important factor in their growth.[9]

LO's current problems stem from the changing structure of the labor force. Many of the better educated members of LO view it as insufficiently responsive to their problems, in part because of its ties to the Labor party:

The LO was always more than just a bargaining agent and a social-democratic club; it has been the key element, along with the Labor Party, of the trade union movement of Norway, and its strength was always partially attributable to a class identity its members felt as workers, and those who made common cause with workers. Although the LO's position in politics had not fundamentally changed in the last 90 years, the concept of class in Norway certainly has. As a social and political group in a modern welfare state, one could say that Norway's laborites are victims of their own success. Joining the LO today simply does not make the same statement about blue-collar working class solidarity that it made 50 years ago.[10]

However, the prevalence of a Labor government during most of the 1980s provided the trade unions with an ideal base for continuing their long reign. They were highly effective in representing the economic interests of their members. Their rating is clearly 5.

SPAIN

The trade unions of Spain are badly split along ideological lines. The General Workers Union, the country's traditional federation, was abolished during the Franco years and emerged when democracy was restored. It is divided internally between factions espousing socialism and those of a more pragmatic bent. It had close ties with the Socialist party, but this alliance weakened during the 1980s when some of its constituent unions opposed policies of the Socialist government.

Its principal rival is the Trade Union Confederation of Workers' Committees (CCOO), formed during the waning years of Franco on the base of officially sponsored works councils. Many councils came under the control of the Communist party, which was behind their consolidation into CCOO. However, a split in the party early in the 1980s resulted in a corresponding rupture within CCOO.

There are also several smaller federations. The Union of Workers' Trade Unions (USO) was established in 1960 by Catholic activists and Socialists who disagreed with UGT policies. It is the most conservative of the federations but is not tied to any political party. There are the Solidarity Movement of Basque Workers with significant support in the Basque provinces, the Independent Confederation of Public Servants, and the Independent Confederation of Trade Unions, the result of a merger of four unions representing administrative and professional personnel.

The fragmentation is a serious obstacle to effective union action. Both UGT and CCOO are represented in most large enterprises and many smaller ones as well. Local bargaining is carried on mainly by elected staff representatives and works committees, both of which are chosen largely from lists of candidates sponsored by the unions. In order for an agreement negotiated by any union to apply to all the employees in the bargaining unit, the union must represent an absolute majority of staff representatives or works committees members. Otherwise, the agreement covers its members only, a formula not designed to maximize union power. Collective agreements at the enterprise level are largely confined to wages, and even there they are limited by national tripartite agreements that set fixed timetables for wage increases.

The unions depend on the government for a large proportion of their financial resources, paid out of the *patrimonio sindical,* trade union funds that had been confiscated under the Franco regime plus accumulated interest. The level of union dues is low, and they are paid by a bare majority of members. The unions are thus unable to render much in the way of services or to finance strikes. Female membership in UGT is only about 10 percent of the total, although by recent estimates women constituted one-quarter of the labor force. Neither UGT nor CCOO have had much success in recruiting white-collar employees.

A recent study summarizes the status of Spanish unionism as follows: "All in all, despite the institutional recognition of its legitimacy, Spanish trade unionism is in a subordinate position, which is due more to a combination of economic factors and internal weaknesses than to the action of anti-labor political or social forces."[11] However, the unions are independent of employer and government control, although subject to influence from allied political parties. Taking into account the fact that they have been operating under a more or less pro-union national government, a rating of 3 seems justified. This is a close call, for they fall perilously near the definition of a category 2 movement. But as one observer put it, "The last decade of democracy has provided the trade unions with an excellent opportunity, within certain constraints, to exert their influence in all fields, and for the most part they have done so admirably."[12]

SWEDEN

The Swedish labor movement occupies a top place in the world's free trade union league by virtue of membership density and status within the country's society. It has problems, but these are of a different order than those confronting most other labor movements. A situation in which female density is 88 percent compared with 82 percent for men, and in which density for public-sector employees is 81 percent, represents union saturation.

The Confederation of Swedish Trade Unions (LO) was founded 100 years ago. In alliance with the Social Democratic party, it was responsible for the transformation of Sweden from a poor agricultural society, exporting mainly people, into a welfare state. It is a fairly centralized organization in that it bargains directly on matters of national importance and can intervene in negotiations conducted by its affiliates. Its sanction must be secured for strikes involving more than 3 percent of the members of an affiliated union contemplating a strike.

Despite its efforts, the LO did not succeed in organizing most white-collar employees. This job was done by a separate federation, the Central Organization of Salaried Employees (TCO), with a membership somewhat more than half of LO's in 1990. TCO is less centralized than LO; it operates primarily as a coordinating and information agency. However, it can represent its entire membership on matters that are of national significance. Its diversity is reflected in the names of its three largest affiliates: the Union of Technical and Clerical Employees in Industry, the National Union of Local Government Officers, and the Federation of Civil Servants. Among its other affiliates are unions of bank employees, police officers, and supervisors. It is politically neutral.

Professionals opted for a third federation, the Confederation of Professional Associations (SACO), the membership of which is 15 percent that of LO's. Many of its 25 national affiliates include people who would not ordinarily be considered good union prospects, including architects and interior designers, lawyers, social scientists and economists, military officers, clergy, pharmacists, scientists, physicians, dentists, and veterinarians. It is also politically neutral.

In many countries, these occupational groups form associations that do engage in some form of bargaining, but they are not usually federated in a centralized body that can speak for all if the necessity arises. SACO is a full-fledged trade union in the sense that it can and does engage in work stoppages. It is this thorough organization of the labor market that makes Swedish unionism unique and explains its extraordinary density ratio.

The unions benefit from a comprehensive network of labor and social legislation, stipulating, among other things, a variant of German codetermination, a high level of job security, and a comprehensive system of training. The social services provided by the government include a national health system, free education up to the university level, and a generous pension scheme that guarantees retirees about two-thirds of the income earned during the last 15 years of their employment, fully indexed.

Sweden has been famous for a centralized collective bargaining model in which the government, unions, and employers attempted to regulate labor market conditions on a national basis in the interest of stability and growth. This model broke down in 1989 when rising wages led to price inflation. Among the political consequences was the defeat of the Social Democrats in the 1991 elections. The new government began to reduce public-sector jobs and to supplement some government services with private alternatives, but it is unlikely that the basic framework of the welfare state will be altered.

In 1988, for the first time in its modern history, LO membership decreased slightly and fell another 0.7 percent in 1989, which it regained in 1990. On the other hand, SACO's membership rose in both 1989 and 1990, while TCO, which had lost members in the previous two years, gained in both 1989 and 1990. However, these were marginal changes and did not represent any real redistribution of union power. Structural employment shifts may alter relative union strength in the future, but with such complete organization, the labor movement as a whole is highly unlikely to be confronted with a challenge to its position in Swedish society. An effectiveness rating of 5 is an obvious conclusion.

UNITED KINGDOM

The British labor movement is the oldest in the world. It has avoided a split along ideological or religious lines, although there is a wide spectrum of views within the Trades Union Congress (TUC), the single federation. The unions created the Labour party in 1905 and have backed it ever since. The current problems faced by the unions stem in part from the alliance.

There were 309 unions registered with the Government Certification Office in 1989, 74 of which were affiliated with TUC. However, this included 83 percent of all union members, some of them in large units, particularly the Transport and General Workers' Union and the General, Municipal, and Boilermakers' Union, both of which cater to employees in a wide variety of industries. The unions were formed in the late nineteenth century in reaction to the elitist policy of unions of skilled craftspeople. Still in existence are a number of small craft unions, but their numbers are diminishing due to financial stringency.

The weak side of the British unions stems from structural and bargaining aspects that antedate the 1980s. The concept of exclusive representation rights for the majority union in a single bargaining unit does not prevail in Britain. Instead, an employer may be obliged to deal with several unions that may even compete for employees with similar jobs and skills. One consequence was the rise of shop stewards' committees elected by employees outside the formal union structure. The committees handled shop floor grievances and were largely responsible for the numerous brief strikes that plagued industrial relations. In 1987, for example, 43 percent of all strikes lasted less than one day, and an additional 34 percent were of one to five days' duration. There is evidence that this practice was somewhat changed during the 1980s.[13] The Employment Act of 1990 was designed to curb wildcat strikes. It made unions liable for damages if any union official called unofficial strikes and allowed an employer to dismiss employees participating in such strikes.

Some unions have attempted to limit multiple representation, but they have run up against tradition. Two conservative organizations, the Engineers and Electrical Unions, entered into agreements giving them exclusive bargaining rights in new or existing plants and were accused of violating the principle of free collective bargaining. The Electricians were also criticized for colluding with the Murdoch newspaper chain against striking printers, leading to their expulsion from TUC.

There has been a recent focus on the role of women both as union officers and members. The density ratio of women was 33 percent in 1989, a decline of 10 percent over the previous decade. However, male density fell by 27 percent during the same decade, so that the greater adherence of women served to mitigate the overall decline.

What was the status of the British unions at the close of the 1980s? "British unions will retain a power and a presence in the British economy: uneven, illogically structured and excessively decentralized as always, rather weaker than before but of continuing importance. It is at the national political level, where their own scope for initiative is weak and where they face the government in Europe most hostile to trade unions, that their fall from the influential years of the 1970s has been most dramatic and where continuing decline seems most likely."[14]

It should be added that the British unions have an advantage that is not available to unions in many other countries. The persistence of class consciousness among manual workers makes it difficult for employers to recruit strikebreakers. All things considered, the British unions merit a rating of 4, if only for their survival as an effective economic force despite their treatment by the Conservative government during the 1980s.

THE UNITED STATES

The trade union situation in the United States is one of the most puzzling. The national unions are united in one central federation, the AFL-CIO. They are well financed, their leaders are well paid, and trade union office provides a desirable career path. Funds are available for organizational work when an opportunity presents itself. Yet the labor movement has experienced a large and unanticipated decline.

Much has been written on the causes of the decline, but no consensus has emerged.[15] Among the hypotheses that have been advanced are structural changes in industry, adverse government attitudes and policies (particularly since 1980), heightened employer opposition, negative public opinion, inappropriate political alliances, failure to appreciate the major concerns of employees, and inadequate attention to the problems of minorities. It has also been argued that the failure to disaggregate the density data conceals the ebb and flow of membership among individual unions. Leo Troy, the dean of U.S. trade union membership analysts, maintains that by dividing the labor force into public and private sectors and looking at individual union densities, an important clue to the decline is revealed.[16]

The problem with these and other explanations is that looking around the world, contradictory evidence can be found. It is easy to cite Reagan-Bush and Thatcher in support of government anti-unionism, but what about Hawke and Mitterand? Structural changes in industry are by no means unique to the United States. Favorable public opinion about unions is not inconsistent with union decline.

What can be said of American unions on the favorable side is, first, that they have been unified for 35 years. There is a diversity of views inside the AFL-CIO. Its constituent unions have more freedom than in most countries to formulate their own policies, but in recent years there has been virtual unanimity on matters of fundamental interest to the labor movement. Union structure is logical and sound; fewer than 100 national unions are affiliated with the AFL-CIO. Local unions are subject to oversight by national unions, and the larger ones are headed by professional executives. There is a substantial union bureaucracy, including lawyers, journalists, economists, and educators. The unions can communicate with their members by newspapers, magazines, radio, and television.

American unions have not been particularly aggressive in attempting to attract workers by catering to concerns not immediately connected with their jobs, but they have been active recently in this area. Among the programs initiated during the last decade are the offer of credit cards at favorable interest rates and the provision of legal and specialized health services.

Foremost on the negative side is the aura of corruption that surrounds some unions and reflects on the movement as a whole. Twenty-five years ago, a committee of the United States Senate held extensive hearings on union governance, in the course of which it was revealed that a number of union officials were using the treasuries of their organizations as their personal property and that some unions had been infiltrated by criminal gangs. Exhibit one was the largest union in the country, the Teamsters, headed by a succession of men who either went to prison for their actions or would have done so if they had not died. The Teamsters were expelled from the AFL-CIO (they have since been reinstated), but the taint remained in the public mind. It was not until 1991 that the federal government stepped in and supervised an election that led to the installation of a reform candidate as union president. Corruption is by no means unique to American unionism, but it has been highly publicized.

While there is no rivalry at the federation level, there is frequently competition for members among national unions. Jurisdictional claims change with the introduction of new technology, but some unions have sought to organize workers in industries and occupations that have little connection with their charters. Jurisdictional work stoppages are largely a thing of the past in part because of legislation but also because the AFL-CIO has established a mechanism for settling them by arbitration.

Union political action is also a factor in judging effectiveness. In its early history, the labor movement followed a policy of "reward your friends, punish your enemies." The old AF of L remained neutral in presidential elections but endorsed candidates of both major parties in state and local elections, depending on their voting records. Since 1948, the AF of L and the CIO and, after unity, the combined federation, backed every Democratic presidential candidate except one whom they regarded as too far to the left. It has been argued that a return to neutrality might be profitable, but the pro-employer tilt of the Republican administrations made this difficult. The unions still back an occasional Republican for Congress and more for local office, but unions are identified with the Democratic party.

On most counts, U.S. trade unions have provided effective service to their members. They are better led, better financed, and better structured than their counterparts in most other nations. Even in the face of government hostility, on the basis of their own internal strength they merit a rating of 5. Despite rising employer opposition, they have continued to be effective representatives of the economic interests of their members in declining industries and have succeeded in organizing several expanding service employment sectors, including government, health, and education.

ARGENTINA

The 1980s were years of change for the labor movement of Argentina. As noted previously, until 1983 the military government that had seized power in 1976 followed a policy of curbing the unions that had been shaped during the regimes of Juan Perón. The central federation, the General Confederation of Labor (CGT), was dissolved, and the right to bargain and strike was suspended.

Beginning in 1982, the government gradually released its hold on the unions. The strike was legalized, as were the rights to carry on normal activities and political action. CGT reorganized, and after some factional struggles it was established as a single umbrella organization. But unity did not last long. Saul Ubaldini, who advocated a militant stand against the government, became secretary general of CGT. He was opposed by a more conciliatory group of the larger industrial unions headed by Lorenzo Miguel that signed an agreement with the Alfonsin government promising no confrontation in return for direct negotiations. One aim of the government was to eliminate the Peronist leadership in the unions, but in this it did not succeed. One reason was that the Miguel faction was also Peronist in outlook. Any movement in this direction was further blocked by the victory of the Peronist presidential candidate in the general elections of 1989.

Factional struggle within CGT weakened the ability of the unions to function independently. Few were able to keep wages moving up with the endemic inflation that prevailed, despite the restoration of bargaining rights. Most unions are industrial in scope and are fairly well financed. Collective bargaining is conducted largely between national unions and employer associations rather than at the enterprise level.

The trade union movement has played an important role in Argentina, at least before 1976 and since 1983. Its vitality when military suppression was lifted attests to its staying power. The principal limitation has been loyalty to the Peronist ideology, although this does not appear to have affected its organizational ability. Had the Justicialist (Peronist) party gained power in 1989 rather than 1983, a rating of 5 would probably have been in order. A rating of 4 is appropriate in light of actual events.

BRAZIL

The Brazilian labor scene, like that of Argentina, underwent drastic changes during the 1980s. The first half of the decade was characterized by the remnants of legal restrictions on unions that had been in effect for 20 years under military rule. Most restrictions were lifted during the second half and the unions were permitted to function independent of the government.

Workers were displaying militancy even before 1985. In 1978, for example, a major strike of metal workers in São Paulo spread to other states. The government did not intervene, and substantial wage increases were negotiated. In 1981, in the face of a legal prohibition against a permanent labor federation, a national meeting, attended by more than 5,000 delegates representing 1,092 unions from all over the country (the First National Conference of the Working Class), resolved to establish a national federation. However, there were two factions among the delegates, both favoring a reform of labor legislation but split on ideology. A more radical faction, which included the Communist party, favored a decentralized federation built from the bottom up, while a conservative faction proposed that the existing official unions be taken over wherever possible.

Two years later, the Central Union of Workers (CUT) was formed by a Congress of Workers, but it soon divided. The radical faction withdrew, held a separate congress, and formed a rival federation, the National Coordination of the Working Class (CONCLAT), leading to a permanent schism in the labor movement. The two federations were under the influence of different political parties, CUT mainly of the Workers party, and CONCLAT, which became the General Workers Confederation (CGT) in 1986, of the country's two main communist parties. Both CUT and CGT soon became embroiled in new internal controversy. CUT managed to hold together and by 1990 had become the nation's dominant federation, while CGT suffered some defections.

Despite a bewildering series of organizational changes, the labor movement managed to attain some stability by the end of the decade. An official of the U.S. Embassy summed up the labor position in the following terms: "Labor's political image in Brazil, as molded by media perceptions, fixed on the CGT's internal fights, the CUT's supposed radicalism, and the propensity of unions everywhere to call strikes at the drop of a hat. . . . Those looking for evidence of irresponsibility in labor's ranks will not have difficulty finding examples. . . . The fact remains that radicalism and irresponsibility characterize the labor movement's fringes, not its mainstream. In the mainstream, the qualities that predominate are sobriety and professionalism."[17]

Brazil's unions are still in a state of transition from 20 years in the shadows. They remain disunited, with the strike weapon as their principal modus operandi. Given the turmoil that characterized the second half of the decade, a rating of 2 would seem appropriate.

CHILE

The Chilean labor movement is one of the oldest in Latin America. Before the military coup in 1973, it enjoyed a density ratio of 37 percent. It led a meager existence during the Pinochet regime but managed to survive and emerged a force to be reckoned with when a democratic government gained power in 1990.

The precoup federation, the Unified Workers Central, was dissolved in 1973, but other groups remained in existence, led by men who were to play a leading role many years later, including Manuel Bustos, who had European support, and Eduardo Rios, who was close to the AFL-CIO. When the state of siege was lifted in 1985 under international pressure, three federations were formed, joining together in 1988 in the Unified Workers Central (CUT), which became the country's leading labor organization, with more than half of all unionists in its ranks. Its leadership included men allied to the Christian Democratic party, the Socialist party, and the Communist party. The noncommunists argued that it was necessary to include the latter to avoid rivalry.

Another federation, the Democratic Workers Central (CDT), headed by Rios, opposed any collaboration with the Communists. It was active in the events that led to Pinochet's loss of a plebiscite in 1988 and his subsequent withdrawal from the presidency. CDT split in 1990 over the refusal of Rios to endorse the electoral platform of Patricio Aylwin, who was victorious. Rios believed that unions should remain independent of political parties. Another federation, the Chilean Workers' Central (CTCH), was formed in 1989 and included leaders who had cooperated with the Pinochet government.

Despite their fragmentation, the Chilean unions did provide workers in key industries with some degree of protection during the 1980s. A general strike in 1985 tied up most of the country's ports, attesting to worker militancy in the face of severe penalties. Collective bargaining picked up toward the end of the Pinochet regime, as did union membership. The number of collective agreements signed rose by 66 percent from 1988 to 1989, and during 1990 union density rose from 10 to 13 percent.

Determining a ranking for the Chilean labor unions during the 1980s is not easy. They regained their independence of government but were handicapped by continuing ideological divisions. Taking into consideration the course of the entire decade, a rating of 2 seems appropriate, although a higher ranking might have been justified had they been more unified and had more time to get organized under a democratic regime.

EGYPT

The scope of the Egyptian labor movement is limited by the fact that only about 5 percent of the nonagricultural labor force is employed in the formal private sector. This means that membership is overwhelmingly in the public sector, particularly because many private firms are not unionized.

There is only one national federation, the Egyptian Trade Union Federation, to which the 25 national unions are required to belong. The government sets wages for its employees and minimum wages in the private sector, so there is little room for independent collective bargaining. Public-sector strikes are banned by law, but in return those employed in this sector have what amounts to permanent employment. Even private firms find it difficult to discharge employees without a lengthy termination process. The unions are committed to the resolution of labor disputes through the courts.

The degree of control over the unions exercised by the Egyptian government calls their ability to act independently into question. Their effect on wages and working conditions does not appear to have been substantial. A rating of 2 best describes their situation.

INDIA

The size of this country and the traditions of the labor market make an assessment of its labor movement complicated. The central labor bodies are divided along ideological lines and tied to different political parties. Securing adequate financing is a difficult problem for them.

These factors contribute to weakness, but nevertheless the Indian unions are quite important.

The largest federation is the Indian National Trade Union Congress (INTUC). Established in 1947, it is allied with the Congress party, which has dominated the political scene for most of the years since independence. INTUC and its affiliates tend to follow a moderate policy based upon Gandhian precepts. Second is the Bharatiya Mazdoor Sangh (BMS), formed in 1955 by Jan Sangh, a militant nationalist political party. One of its principal goals was to reduce communist influence in the labor movement. Its main strength is among white-collar employees.

Hind Mazdoor Sangh is a third federation, socialist in orientation and centered in the transportation and steel industries and in the plantations. The nation's oldest federation, the All India Trade Union Congress (AITUC), is controlled by the Communist party of India, which was oriented toward the former Soviet Union, while the Center of Indian Trade Unions (CITU) is the trade union wing of the pro–Chinese Marxist Communist party. The National Labor Organization (NLO) is an offshoot of the venerable Textile Labor Association, which was founded by Gandhi but has been losing members because of the decline of the textile industry.

The fragmentation has had negative effects on the labor movement. There is considerable competition among affiliates at the local level. An employer may have to deal with a multiplicity of unions with varying demands. There are financial problems, compounded by low wages and interunion competition with low dues as an attraction. The checkoff and union shop are illegal, so dues are not paid regularly.

Yet Indian unions can be effective bargainers, and many are quite militant. Strikes are frequent. In 1989, for example, month-long strikes closed universities, hospitals, and other public institutions. There were stoppages at automobile plants, shoe factories, jute mills, and other manufacturing enterprises. Although the unions are under strong political party influence, they are independent of government control. Their appropriate classification is 3.

KENYA

All but two of Kenya's major trade unions have been affiliated with the Central Organization of Trade Unions (COTU), the only labor federation in the country. There once were two independents, the National Union of Teachers and the Union of Civil Servants; the latter was ordered by the government to withdraw from COTU in 1969. The government has dominated labor-management relations and the unions as well.

The Civil Service Union was dissolved by presidential decree in 1980. To convince the International Labour Organization that civil servants did not lose their right to representation, the Civil Service Association was formed two years later, but it never secured a significant membership. The teachers were threatened with similar treatment, but they managed to retain their union status.

There have been strikes, particularly from 1986 to 1988. Most were short and arose from local issues. The government has imposed wage guidelines, limiting wage increases to 75 percent of the inflation rate. COTU has raised objections to this policy but to no avail.

Although COTU has a monopoly position in Kenyan unionism, it is divided along the tribal lines that permeate Kenyan society. The Luos have accused the secretary general of COTU, a Luhya, of attempting to bar them from leadership positions, while the various factions have been trading allegations of misappropriation of union funds. Despite considerable dissatisfaction with the political system, COTU has continued to back the government. At one time, Kenya had a vigorous labor movement under the guidance of Tom Mboye, the best-known labor leader that Africa has produced. Since his assassination, COTU has declined as an independent organization. Its rating is 2.

KOREA

The position of Korea's trade unions during the decade of the 1980s changed drastically in 1987. Before that, the only central labor body was the Federation of Korean Trade Unions (FKTU), operating under government control. Roh, who won the presidency in 1987, promised that he would change the system. "Roh's speech was like a match set to timber waiting to be kindled. It provided the opportunity for unionism to explode out of the confines in which it had been shackled. Decades of pent up humiliations were let loose resulting in wave after wave of worker demonstrations and union organizing."[18]

The upshot of this burst of union activity was the reinvigoration of the FKTU and the end of its monopoly position. It remains the largest federation, consisting of 20 affiliates. However, it is split between a more liberal wing concentrated in manufacturing and more conservative groups elsewhere. It has become much more independent than it was before 1987, but it is committed to working within the social system.

A more radical group arose from the strike wave in opposition to the FKTU. In January 1990, many newly established unions joined in establishing the National Labor Alliance, but the government condemned it as illegal and its membership was halved. A second attempt at federation later in the year resulted in a loose organization, the Solidarity Conference of Large Company Unions. Other unions have remained independent of both the FKTU and the Solidarity Conference.

The trade unions are handicapped by rivalry and by frequent government intervention in collective bargaining. Some union leaders were arrested for illegal organizational efforts when they were refused registration. The government has been concerned with restraining wages and set an example by limiting wage increases in the public sector. One result of intervention has been a sharp decline in strikes, which fell by 80 percent from 1989 to 1990. Wages nonetheless continued to rise during 1989, and labor costs increased by 21 percent and by 17 percent the following year. Even more important, hours of work fell from what had been one of the highest levels in the world to 48 hours a week in 1990.

Not all of this can be attributed to union pressure. A booming economy, inflation, and labor shortages contributed to a tight labor market in which unemployment remained low. However, union militancy, particularly on the part of the new unions, suggests that the unions did play a significant role in raising living standards. Had they been united, they might have been even more effective, but as things stood, and taking into account the predemocratic years, they should be rated at a level of 3. While government policy remained an obstacle to organization even after the 1987 breakthrough, it was of a completely different degree from that which had prevailed earlier.

MALAYSIA

The Malaysian labor movement has operated under handicaps that restricted their expansion, particularly racial divisions and strict government regulation. All new unions are required to register and can be denied registration if "there is already in existence a trade union in respect of the particular trade, occupation, or industry, and if it is not in the interest of the workmen concerned that there be another trade union of a similar character." General or multi-industrial unions are effectively barred. The legal requirement does have the virtue, however, of preventing competitive bidding for members.

The dominant national federation is the Malaysian Trade Union Congress (MTUC). In 1990, its 145 affiliates had 500,000 members, about 70 percent of the country's organized workers. There are also a federation of public-sector unions with 120,000 members and a new central body, the Malaysian Labor Organization (MLO), organized in 1989 under the leadership of bank employees, with 100,000 members.

Company-based unions have been encouraged in government enterprises, and by 1990, almost 250,000 employees were represented by these unions. But despite the government's preference for company unions, new ones were refused registration where organization already existed. A bargaining problem facing all unions is the power of the minister of Human Resources to refer disputes to compulsory arbitration by the Industrial Court, and as a result there are few strikes.

The largest national union in the country is the National Union of Plantation Workers, the membership of which fell from 120,000 in 1980 to 78,000 in 1991. Were it not for this, overall union density would have risen over the decade. The decline has been attributed to the increased use of temporary contract workers on the plantations, to the conversion of some plantations to the production of less labor-intensive palm oil, and to urban housing that has spread to the countryside. Apart from its size, the plantation union has also enjoyed prestige because of the reputation of its founder and secretary general for many years, P. P. Narayanan, who has been president of the International Confederation of Free Trade Unions and is one of the best-known union leaders in Asia.

Why have the seemingly well-established unions of Malaysia been able to enroll only about 10 percent of the country's employees? The small size of the average enterprise is one answer. Government encouragement of company unions is another. If the membership of the company unions were included, the density rate would have been 13 percent in 1989, not an unduly low figure for a developing country. Sharp ethnic divisions are another explanation; 47 percent of the population is Malay, 34 percent Chinese, 9 percent Indian, and the rest non–Malay tribes. Government programs designed to raise the incomes of Malays have aroused resentment among the others and made cooperation difficult. The unions, both leaders and members, are predominantly Malay.

Within the organized sectors, and despite government regulation, the unions have not done badly for their members. Collective bargaining is the norm, and grievances are processed effectively. Although the labor movement is divided, jurisdictional lines are clear and interunion rivalry does not appear to be debilitating. Malaysia has one of the few labor movements in south Asia that has achieved a solid status of legitimacy through years of activity. A rating of 3 would appear to be justified.

MEXICO

The trade union situation in Mexico is unique. The main trade union body is part of the political party that dominates the government. The unions play an important role in the political decision-making process, and the political party with which it is allied has elected every president and most state and congressional candidates since 1929. The organization that occupies this position is the Confederation of Mexican Workers (CTM). Its influence is extended through its control of a loose coordinating body, the Congress of Labor, which includes independent unions and federations as well as CTM.

The only other federation of any substantial size is the Federation of Government Employee Unions. Several other federations are either regional or leftovers from past ideological struggles. Several umbrella organizations that include splinter leftist parties as well as unions offer the only union opposition to the dominant party of Revolutionary Institutions (PRI).

Can a trade union in the position occupied by PRI do a reasonably good job for its members? Mexico has been struggling against inflation and seeking to raise industrial productivity, goals that may run counter to the immediate interests of workers, who want higher wages and more employment security in the short run. Challenges to government policy have come mainly from non–CTM unions, but some criticism of Fidel Velazquez, the long-time head of CTM, has arisen even within CTM. Real wages in manufacturing fell during the 1980s, reflecting a lack of worker militancy. "By controlling worker demands, the labor movement has contributed decisively to the industralization and capital accumulation process in years when the country experienced growth rates in excess of six percent per year for almost three decades."[19] CTM was obliged to become more militant during the 1980s because of economic difficulties: inflation, currency devaluation, and a foreign debt crisis. "Nevertheless, the direct ties to the state and the subordination to the latter's economic policies have not substantially changed."[20]

Mexico's unions are the strongest in Latin America. This is a major achievement in a country in which unemployment may run as high as 20 percent and where thousands of workers are forced to seek dubious economic opportunities in the United States. Staying organized has not been a problem, and the ruling party is not likely to weaken one of its main electoral assets by adopting policies that endanger union stability. The rating of the Mexican unions is 5.

THE PHILIPPINES

The Philippine unions were under the thumb of the government until democracy was restored with the ousting of Marcos in 1986. They were rejuvenated during the rest of the decade, but sharp divisions among competing groups hampered their development and growth. A lagging economy and heavy unemployment added to their difficulties.

The largest union center is the Trade Union Congress of the Philippines (TUCP), with 40 national affiliates. The Federation of Free Workers and the Manggagawa Labor Center were smaller organizations that joined in a loose coalition with TUCP. Opposed to TUCP was the May First Movement (KMU), which headed a smaller conglomerate, the Labor Advisory and Consultative Council.

TUCP and KMU remain at the opposite poles of the labor movement. TUCP, which is branded a "yellow" union by the left, favors cooperation with employers in the interests of economic development. KMU calls for militant action and has been involved in numerous strikes that are out of proportion to its membership. There are also many local unions without any national affiliation.

Industrial relations improved during the final years of the 1980s. Strikes declined steadily after the heady days following the installation of the Aquino regime, and genuine collective bargaining became more common. The principal drawback to satisfactory union organization has been the intense rivalry among the unions, often tinged with violence. The various factions did manage to cooperate in 1990 to protest a large increase in the price of fuel and to demand an increase in the minimum wage. When President Aquino appealed for a withdrawal of a general strike threat, KMU refused and called the strike, leading to violence and the deaths of six people. The other unions met with Aquino and received a package of nonwage benefits that satisfied them temporarily.

Given low density and fragmentation, the Philippine unions cannot be regarded as effective. The failure to build a consensus after years of oppression and the continuation of serious rivalry indicate that a rating of 2 is appropriate.

TAIWAN

The Chinese Federation of Labor (CFL) languished under the strict control of the Kuomintang, Taiwan's governing party, until 1987. Its affiliates were grievance processors rather than bargaining agents. Only with the lifting of martial law in 1987 did unions with some degree of independence emerge. Several new unions were established, and in some of the older unions, officially sponsored candidates for union office were defeated. An initial burst of strikes ended in union victories, but a stoppage of bus drivers in August 1988 was terminated when the government held it illegal. Employers were emboldened to resist union demands, and several strikes against large employers ended in defeat for the unions. "The independent labor movement which exploded after the lifting of martial law in July 1987 reached a high point in 1989 and then rapidly lost momentum. . . . Although mass leaves and work stoppages continued to be used throughout the year, they became less frequent as many workers recognized the limitations on their power."[21]

The expansion of unionism in Taiwan is hampered by a law that prohibits competing labor federations in any administrative district, including cities, counties, and the country itself. This means that there can be only one Taiwan-wide labor federation, and it restricts any opposition to small units.

The Kuomintang still appears to have a great deal of influence over CFL policy. CFL argues that its effectiveness is enhanced by close relationships with government officials. Union density did rise substantially during the decade, particularly during the last few years. It rose from 23 to 30.5 percent from 1987 to 1989. About 75 percent of CFL members are in the Taipei area, where a large portion of the country's economic activity is concentrated. A substantial proportion of the growth is the result of self-employed workers who are joining unions to participate in publicly subsidized labor insurance programs.

Taiwan's labor movement is in transition. Political democracy has been strengthened and with it the prospect of fully independent unionism. As of 1990, however, "the evidence is quite strong that the CFL still operates basically as an extension of the KMT [Kuomintang]."[22] A rating of 2 is appropriate.

THAILAND

The Thai labor movement has been battered by a succession of military governments. It has a density rate lower than any labor movement in this study and is highly fragmented. The unions were already split in 1988 when the first elected government in 12 years came into office. The next three years of civilian rule, terminated by a military coup, did not see much improvement. By 1990, there were four federations and three looser congresses. Because about half of all employees in Thailand work for a public enterprise, the largest organization is the State Enterprise Labor Relations Group, a coalition of public-sector employees. The labor movement received a body blow in 1991 when the state enterprise unions were dissolved and replaced by associations with little power.

Contributing to the split in the labor movement were tensions between the public- and private-sector unions. Some centers had been affiliated with political parties, but by 1988 they had proclaimed their neutrality. However, many union officials maintained close relationships with government officials and were the recipients of special favors, which others resented. Four union presidents were appointed to the National Legislative Assembly after the 1991 coup.

The unions failed to take advantage of the short period during the last few years of the 1980s in which they could operate with relative in-

Table 5.1
Trade Union Effectiveness (Ratings 1 to 5)

Industrial Countries		Developing Countries	
Australia	5	Argentina	4
Canada	4	Brazil	2
Denmark	5	Chile	2
France	3	Egypt	2
Germany	5	India	3
Italy	3	Kenya	2
Japan	3	Korea	3
New Zealand	4	Malaysia	3
Norway	5	Mexico	5
Spain	3	Philippines	2
Sweden	5	Taiwan	2
United Kingdom	4	Thailand	2
United States	5		

Code:
1. Unions banned or under complete government control
2. Employers favored by government
3. Government neutral between labor and management
4. Unions favored by government
5. Government strongly pro-union

dependence. The main cause seems to have been disunity. To achieve a more satisfactory status, they will have to overcome the centrifugal forces that have separated them. The rating for the decade is 2.

SUMMARY

The trade union effectiveness ratings are summarized in Table 5.1. There does appear to be some relationship between union effectiveness and density for the industrial countries, although not for the developing countries. The correlation coefficient emerging from a regression involving the industrial countries is 0.26, significant at the 4 percent level. Effectiveness is the only variable thus far considered, apart from unemployment, that has some explanatory power for this group of countries. What appears to be true is that where unions were more united, better structured, and with superior political connections, they were more able to hold their members – although there were some conspicuous exceptions. That there is no clear relationship for the developing countries does not mean that union quality was not important for them but that quality was overshadowed by other factors.

NOTES

1. For a good summary, see Richard B. Freeman and James L. Medoff, *What Do Unions Do?* (New York: Basic Books, 1984), ch. 3.

2. D. W. Rawson, *Unions and Unionism in Australia* (Sydney: Allen & Unwin, 1986), p. 41.

3. Rawson, *Unions,* p. 105.

4. Gregor Murray, *Canadian Unions and Economic Restructuring* (Kingston, Ontario, Canada: Queen's University, 1991), p. 14.

5. Pradeep Kumar and Dennis Ryan (eds.), *Canadian Labor Movement in the 1980s* (Kingston, Ontario, Canada: Queen's University, 1988), p. 14.

6. Otto Jacobi and Walter Muller-Jentsch, "Germany," in Guido Baglioni and Colin Crouch, eds., *European Industrial Relations* (London: Sage, 1990), pp. 149–150.

7. Tasiho Shirai, *Contemporary Industrial Relations in Japan* (Madison: University of Wisconsin Press, 1983), pp. 137–138.

8. The foregoing data are from Japan Institute of Labor, *Japanese Working Life in Profile* (Tokyo: Japanese Institute of Labor, 1992), and World Bank, *World Development Report* (Washington, D.C.: World Bank, 1991).

9. Norwegian Federation of Labor, *Temabok,* Oslo, 1991, p. 129..

10. U.S. Department of Labor, *Foreign Labor Trends: Norway, 1989–1991* (Washington, D.C.: GPO), p. 12.

11. Jordi Estivill and Josep M. de la Hoz, "Transition and Crisis," in Baglioni and Crouch, eds., *European Industrial Relations,* p. 286.

12. Roger C. McElrath, *Trade Unions and the Industrial Relations Climate in Spain* (Philadelphia: Wharton School, 1989), p. 124.

13. Richard Hyman, *Strikes* (London: Macmillan, 1989), p. 203.

14. Colin Crouch, "United Kingdom: The Rejection of Compromise," in Baglioni and Crouch, eds., *European Industrial Relations,* p. 354.

15. For a good review of the literature, see Industrial Relations Research Association, *The State of the Unions* (Madison, Wis.: Industrial Relations Research Association, 1991).

16. Leo Troy, "Is the U.S. Unique in the Decline of Private Sector Unionism?" *Journal of Labor Research,* Spring 1990, p. 115.

17. U.S. Department of Labor, *Foreign Labor Trends: Brazil, 1989,* p. 10.

18. George E. Ogle, *Korea: Dissent within the Economic Miracle* (London: Zed Books, 1990), p. 115.

19. Edward C. Epstein, *Labor Autonomy and the State in Latin America* (Boston: Unwin Hyman, 1989), p. 190.

20. Epstein, *Labor Autonomy*, p. 191.
21. U.S. Department of Labor, *Foreign Labor Trends: Taiwan, 1989*, p. 5.
22. Archie Kleingartner and Hseuh-yu Peng, *Taiwan: A Study of Labor Relations in Transition* (Los Angeles: Institute of Industrial Relations, University of California, 1990), p. 14.

Chapter 6

Employer Attitudes

A study of the problems facing trade unions would not be complete without reference to employer attitudes toward organization of workers, particularly because this is often cited as a cause of union decline. There are several difficulties in categorizing employers. There may be wide differences among them, based on personal views or the industries in which they operate. For example, employers in export industries tend to be much tougher in dealing with unions than those producing for the domestic market, because the former are apt to be more concerned than the latter with the effects of rising wages and prices, for competitive reasons.

Also, employers are apt to be strongly influenced and constrained by government attitudes. It is the rare employer who welcomes trade unions into the shop; most would prefer individual bargaining. The degree to which employers' hostility is manifested depends largely on restraints imposed by government policy. Employer attitudes are hardly an independent factor in explaining union decline; faced with a pro-union government, employers are likely to be conciliatory.

Here an attempt is made first to classify prevailing employer attitudes in the industrial countries into three groups: actively hostile toward unions, pragmatic acceptance of union existence, and belief in the value of cooperating with them. Employers in developing countries tend to be more polarized, have typically had less experience in dealing with unions, and often have a great deal of influence over government policy.

An important determinant of employer attitudes is the extent to which employers are organized into associations. The associations are generally staffed by labor relations specialists who have a personal interest in collective bargaining. This does not mean that employer associations cannot be militantly anti-union, but over time their policies soften as collective bargaining becomes routine.

THE INDUSTRIAL COUNTRIES

Cooperative Employers

The Scandinavian employers exemplify those who made peace with the unions many years ago and learned to live with them in a spirit of mutual cooperation. There are occasional work stoppages, strikes, or lockouts, but there is every expectation that when the dispute is settled, either by direct negotiation or through government intervention, labor and management will resume friendly relationships.

The Danish Employers' Association (DAF), which dates from 1899, is composed of 45 branch organizations and a few individual company members, representing 26,000 individual employers. While 75 percent of Danish employers are not in DAF, its agreements largely determine labor conditions in the private sector and to a lesser extent in the public sector. DAF does little collective bargaining, leaving that to its affiliated bodies. An employer who is unwilling to accept the terms agreed to by an association can be fined under breach of contract, because the employer agreed to abide by its decisions upon joining. DAF is well financed and staffed, and among the services it renders its members is representation before a Labor Court when contract grievances cannot be settled by negotiation. This is important, because the Court operates on the principle of stare decisis—its awards constitute precedents for future disputes. DAF's staff of lawyers, economists, and journalists is prepared to provide other services when the need arises.

In 1989, the oldest of the Norwegian employer organizations, the Employers' Association (NAF), joined with formerly independent handicraft and industry groups to form the Central Employers' Association (NHO). The new federation represents 10,000 enterprises, and its agreements with the Federation of Labor cover 225,000 employees. At the time of the merger, the combined associations had 150 separate national affiliates, but this was reduced to 30 in the interest of efficiency. Independent of NHO is the Central Organization of Commercial Employers, the affiliates of which employ 50,000 workers. There are also separate employer organizations in shipping, agriculture, trade, banking, insurance, and private health institutions.

NHO has a staff of 200 in its central administration, and its regional branches employ an additional 55. It bargains on matters of national scope. For example, its predecessor, NAF, entered into an agreement with the government and trade unions to put a 5-percent cap on wages;

in return, the government committed itself to lower interest rates on housing loans, a reduction in the age of retirement, and longer maternity leave. The agreement was imposed on all employees in the country by legislation.

Even when things seem to go wrong, peaceful negotiations usually prevail in the end. In 1990, an agreement between LO and NHO was rejected by the membership of LO, which then threatened a general strike. Government mediation resulted in sweetening the originally agreed-upon wage increase. In return, the unions agreed to a two-year contract during which all strikes would be illegal.

The Swedish Employers' Association (SAF) unites 40,000 member firms employing 30 percent of the labor force. The banks and newspapers have their own associations; there is an independent employer group that bargains for publicly owned companies, and there are separate bodies for dealing with central and local government employees.

SAF has 37 affiliates. The SAF secretariat consists of almost 500 people, with separate sections for research, collective bargaining, statistics, and public relations. Collective bargaining takes place on three levels: SAF deals with LO and the other federations on matters of national importance, its affiliates deal with corresponding national unions, and individual adjustments are made at the level of the enterprise. Unorganized employers generally follow the terms of agreements reached by LO.

The only controversy in recent years that led to a serious breach of good relations involved the establishment in 1983 of so-called wage-earner funds by the government under union pressure. Five regional funds were financed by a tax on profits or payrolls, whichever yielded the greater amount, each governed by a nine-member board that had five union appointees. The funds were to invest primarily in corporate stock, with each fund limited to 8 percent of a single corporation's voting stock. The employers were vehemently opposed to the scheme, branding it "socialism by the back door." When the legislation was debated by Parliament, employers mounted a large demonstration outside, a highly unusual event.

The funds remained controversial for the rest of the decade and were a major issue in the 1991 general elections, which resulted in a defeat for the socialists. One of the first acts of the incoming government was to introduce legislation terminating the funds, which are not likely to be reinstated when the Social Democrats regain power, in part because the experiment "can hardly be construed as a successful model of economic democracy."[1]

While the ideological controversy ruffled the otherwise smooth waters of Swedish industrial relations, collective bargaining continued its normal course. Swedish employers are by no means laggards in defending their economic interests, but they accept unions as an integral part of the country's social fabric.

Scandinavia is in a class by itself when it comes to employer attitudes toward trade unions, but other countries should be added to the list of cooperating employers. One of them is Australia, where employers are neither as well organized nor as centralized as in Scandinavia but nevertheless maintain fairly cordial relations with trade unions. The most representative body is the Confederation of Australian Industry (CAI), which has 40 major affiliates. Alongside it are the Independent Metal Industry Association, the Business Council of Australia (which includes the chief executives of the country's 80 largest firms), and separate federations of employers in Victoria and New South Wales.

Employer organization came about largely as a result of the country's unique system of industrial relations. Disputes over new agreements are subject to compulsory arbitration by federal and state tribunals in the event of negotiating failure. Of particular importance are hearings before the Federal Industrial Relations Commission, which rules on national wage cases. Its awards determine the compensation of about 80 percent of all wage earners.

The CAI was formed in part because of the way the system operates. "Because of the profound impact of National Wage Case decisions on industry's cost structure a large amount of effort goes into preparing for these (currently) twice-year hearings. . . . One of the major objectives in forming the CAI was to avoid the divided opinions which had, from time to time, been presented in hearings before the tribunals. Cohesion is achieved by continuous consultation."[2]

Union legitimacy in Australia is assured by its key role in the bargaining process. There are occasional strikes, although they are technically illegal, and unions that sanction them may be held liable for damages. However, only rarely do companies institute such lawsuits; that is not the way the Australian system operates.

Germany is another country in which employer attitudes have been formed by the structure of industrial relations. Codetermination is the main institutional reason; employees and trade unions are represented on corporate boards of directors, and employees exercise a good deal of power through works councils at the plant level. As many as 90 percent of German employers belong to industrial associations, which are affiliated with a central body, the Federation of German Employer Associations (BDA). Employers were far from enthusiastic about the invasion of their managerial authority, but the union momentum engendered by postwar events gave them little choice.

Unions and employer associations "face each other almost continually at one organizational level or another in the multiemployer bargaining process at the federal and *land* levels. Representatives from each of the two structures sit side by side almost daily in the specialized labor and social courts and in the various quasi-governmental agencies administering social and labor policy. They are, in summary, the two major institutional actors in the West German industrial relations system."[3]

New Zealand also appears to belong with countries of cooperative employers. The New Zealand Employers Federation is a loose association of four regional groups that enjoy considerable autonomy. Almost 40 percent of employers who are members of the various federations are in wholesale and retail trade, and only 10 percent are in manufacturing.

Before 1991, the unions operated in a benign environment characterized by annual negotiations between groups of employers and unions in which minimum wages and other conditions of employment were set for 350 lines of work. The contracts were extended to enterprises that did not participate in the negotiations. Until 1987, either party could invoke compulsory arbitration, but this was changed by legislation requiring the consent of both parties. There was a partial return to the old system in 1990; if an agreement was not reached in two years, and if one of the parties could be shown to have bargained in bad faith, final offer arbitration could be mandated. In general, employers accepted the unions as legitimate partners in the system, although confrontation was not entirely absent.

The scene was altered in 1991 when a conservative government came into power. Among the changes were the exemption from the operation of any agreements that were reached of employers who did not participate in national bargaining. The legislation was strongly supported by the employers federation and opposed by the unions. It was the culmination of the employers' effort to change a system they regarded as contrary to economic efficiency. Had this occurred during the 1980s, there might have been reason to exclude the New Zealand employers from the cooperative category.

Pragmatic Employers

This group consists of employers who do not welcome unions into their plants and might prefer to operate nonunion if it were feasible. They do not seek to break unions, but they are strongly opposed to any dilution of their managerial authority. Most are organized but not as comprehensively as the cooperative employers.

French employers are quite well organized in contrast to the unions with which they deal. The Confederation of French Industries and Services (CNPF) represents 1.5 million companies in 85 professional federations. The CNPF is recognized by the government as the official partner in negotiations, tripartite tribunals, and comanagers with labor in the unemployment and pension systems.

French employers have a long history of antipathy to trade unions that is exacerbated by the control of the largest central union federation by the Communist party. Employers have nevertheless been required to bargain collectively on an annual basis over wages and other conditions of labor and to supply regular information to works committees. In fact, a few large corporations have attempted to prevent the decline of unions within their enterprises on the theory that the disappearance of valid unions would lead to wildcat strikes and a lack of discipline. Among other things, employees were given blank dues checks that could be turned over to the union of their choice.

Most employers continue to believe that unions are basically external to the enterprise and are reluctant to accept them as bargaining partners. The national bargaining that took place during the 1980s was mandated by the government rather than by any desire to create Scandinavian-type labor-management relationships.

Until the widespread strikes of 1968–1969, Italian employers were not willing to accept unions as bargaining partners at the enterprise level. Their principal organization, the General Federation of Italian Industry (Confindustria), consisted at the time of 106 local associations and about 100,000 firms with 3.2 million employees in a labor force of 20 million. Until 1957, Confindustria represented state-owned enterprises as well as those in the private sector, but the former were obliged to withdraw and form a central federation of their own. There are also separate employer bodies in commerce, agriculture, banking, and handicrafts.

During the 1980s, there was a trend toward firm-level bargaining and away from industry bargaining coordinated by Confindustria, but more centralized bargaining persists. As in France, the domination by the Communist party of the General Federation of Italian Labor (CGIL), the largest of the union federations, hampered closer labor-management relationships. The dissolution of the communist faction in CGIL that took place in 1990 may remove this barrier, particularly if the competing union federations are prepared to work together.

For most of the postwar years, Confindustria took a hard line and was generally regarded by the unions as their enemy. But during the 1980s, when Fiat, the largest employer in the country, shifted from cooperation with the unions to strong confrontation, Confindustria became more involved with smaller firms and established good relationships with the socialist-led governments that came into office. The bargaining power of the unions declined, but they made up for it with their growing political role.

Given the center-left complexion of most of the national government administrations, employers have had little option but to deal with the unions within the context of the industrial relations system. This implies an attitude of pragmatism, of a willingness to tolerate the unions rather than seek their destruction. As one analyst put it, "Government and unions together have restrained hard line employers from adopting unilateral strategies to bypass collective bargaining. . . . Confindustria and its affiliates continue to play an important part in labor negotiations at all levels of the industrial relations system."[4]

Canadian employers are not well organized. There is no national employers' association devoted to industrial relations, although there are regional and industry groups. The normal collective bargaining unit is the individual firm rather than an entire industry, although pattern bargaining characterizes the steel and automobile industries.

While employer organization tends to lead to greater accommodation with unions, the individualistic employers of Canada are not necessarily anti-union. There has been bilateral cooperation on specific issues of mutual concern to labor and management. For example, the Canadian Labor Congress and the Business Council on National Issues jointly established the Labor Market and Productivity Center in 1984. Similar organizations are the Steel Trade and Employment Congress, the Sectoral Skills Council in the electronics industry, and the Textile Labor-Management Committee. "Although much of the bilateral consultation and cooperation has revolved around industry restructuring and labor adjustment issues, the joint initiatives have led to enhanced dialogue, greater information sharing, shared beliefs and understanding and identification of mutual goals and objectives."[5]

The diversity of labor relations in Canada makes it difficult to summarize the prevalent attitude of employers toward unions. The following is a brief attempt to do so:

Canadian managers have limited commitment to collective bargaining and formal labor relations. Non-union firms strive to retain that status, some by matching the wages and working conditions in the unionised sector, others by combinations of paternalism and coercion. . . . A great many unionised firms accept the role of labor grudgingly, although open attacks on incumbent unions are rare. But in industries with a long history of unionism – for example, manufacturing or transportation – unionism is accepted as a normal part of the environment.[6]

That is not a bad definition of employer pragmatism.

Spanish employer organization is of relatively recent origin along with the entire system of industrial relations. The Federation of Employers' Organizations (CEOE) was founded in 1977, and while there are independent regional and industry associations, it is the most influential. Originally, the CEOE was a defensive body designed to help employers attain legitimacy after the demise of the Franco regime. It has since established fairly good relations with the socialist governments. Naturally, it tended to favor the socialist-dominated UGT over the more radical CCOO.

CEOE negotiates agreements at the national level, setting a framework for bargaining at the industry and enterprise levels. Large firms tend to sign their own agreements, but almost all small enterprises negotiate on a multi-employer basis. Employers balked on one major issue, a union demand for greater control over temporary work contracts, which cover one-third of total employment. Under union pressure, a law mandating the provision of basic information to unions on all such contracts was enacted in 1991. Apart from this, other issues have been negotiated with relative amity. However, CEOE "has resisted efforts to reduce working time and to include pay revision clauses in collective bargaining agreements, and sought to increase company flexibility in the deployment of the work force."[7] As for general employer attitudes, "as a whole [they] seek not to eliminate unions from industrial relations. . . . This does not mean, of course, that on some occasions and in some companies employers have not sought to bar union participation or sponsored company unions or urged individual employment contracts."[8]

British employers began to organize industry associations as early as the middle of the nineteenth century, but it was not until 1965 that an umbrella organization was formed. This was the Confederation of British Industries (CBI), representing the merger of three large federations. CBI does not engage in collective bargaining; this is done by national associations, 148 of which were listed with the government in 1986, plus some that were not listed. There has been a strong movement toward single-employer agreements during the last two decades, and a number of large firms have withdrawn from their associations to conduct their own bargaining.

Before the Thatcher government, employers maintained good relations with the unions, as a whole. Although the unions were committed to a socialist society, "at varying levels of practical activity . . . a great deal of mutual accommodation has been achieved. CBI representatives take their place with TUC representatives on an extensive range of government-created institutions and independent organizations."[9] There were some union practices to which employers objected strenuously, including the closed shop and the plethora of brief strikes engineered by shop stewards in prosecuting grievances,[10] but regular strikes and lockouts were usually settled by negotiation rather than by eliminating the unions involved.

To what extent did employers share responsibility for the hostile attitude of the Thatcher government? CBI is politically neutral, although there is little doubt that employers are happier with a Conservative than with a Labour government. A study of CBI published in 1977 reached the conclusion that "CBI has little consistent direct influence over the policies pursued by the government [but] it can influence considerably a particular piece of legislation."[11] A study conducted after the Conservatives had been in power for a decade noted that "there is no doubt that the CBI has enjoyed considerably less influence under the Thatcher administration than it expected to have at the time of the Conservative Government's election in 1979."[12]

On the whole, there is little evidence that British employers have sought to eliminate a union presence either through legislation or their own policies. They did push for abolition of what they regarded as egregious union practices, but collective bargaining continued to be the normal method of determining labor conditions.

Hostile Employers

There is a real question of whether Japanese employers should be classified as hostile. Japanese experts are almost unanimous in the view that employers are pro-union, as exemplified by the support they accord the enterprise-level organizations that are almost universal in Japan.

Employers in Japan are joined in the Federation of Employer Associations (Nikkerein), which consists of 8 regional associations and 55 industrial associations, to which 31,000 corporations adhere (1990). Nikkerein does not engage directly in collective bargaining, although it does attempt to develop general guidelines for the annual wage settlement. The same is true of the industry associations, although they are believed to play an informal role in coordinating the responses of the major firms to the annual union demands.

It is important to note that union membership is concentrated in the larger firms. In 1991, the unionization rate was 58.7 percent in firms with 1,000 or more regular employees, 23.3 percent in firms with 100 to 1,000 employees, and 1.8 percent in firms with fewer than 100 employees.[13] Many unorganized firms have alternative organizations called *shainkai* to provide a mechanism for employer-employee communication. According to a recent survey, 75 percent of employee representatives in the union sector hold managerial positions above the section chief level, compared with 60 percent in the nonunion sector. The survey concluded that "although some *shainkai* serve as alternative to unions, it is not so clear that all of the *shainkai* really reflect the workers' interests. In some cases, existence of the *shainkai* may prevent workers from organizing unions, while in other cases the *shainkai* actually developed into unions."[14]

Smaller firms do not welcome unions, and few are organized. The problem with evaluating the attitudes of the large firms lies in the nature of the enterprise unions. Employers are not only friendly with these unions but have a major stake in their continued existence. If the balance of union power were to shift from the enterprise to the national level, Japanese labor relations would probably become much more confrontational and hostile, as they were during the 1960s, when some large national strikes were mounted. As it is, they are happy with the current arrangement, as employers anywhere would be if faced only with local unions that they could control. Japanese employers are certainly cooperative with their company unions but show little liking for the largely ineffective national unions with which they are not required to deal.

As for the United States, most American employers have never voluntarily accepted collective bargaining as a normal process. The large corporations were forced by the federal government to recognize unions during the Great Depression and World War II. The business community gradually drifted toward a confrontational position beginning with the Eisenhower years, but the real drive came in 1980 with the famous strike of the air traffic controllers, when Ronald Reagan, newly installed as president, discharged all the strikers and replaced them with military personnel and civilian recruits, destroying the union. The action was taken in accordance with federal legislation banning strikes by government employees, but it had never been enforced in so drastic a fashion.

There have been numerous industry-level employer associations but no nationwide federation. Many associations were local and typically involved small employers who organized to deal with powerful unions. Construction, trucking, retail trade, food, and apparel were examples. The larger employers in automobiles, electrical manufacturing, and other mass production industries preferred to bargain directly with the unions. The major business associations, the National Association of Manufacturers and the Chamber of Commerce, were not involved in industrial relations. An employer organization dedicated to the elimination of the union shop, the National Right to Work Committee, was able to secure legislation that achieved this purpose in almost half the states.

The 1980s witnessed the most sustained anti-union drive since the years following World War I. Firms specializing in helping employers establish a "union-free environment" planned strategies for defeating union organizing drives and dislodging them where they existed. Industrial restructuring shrank some major industries in which unions had been strong and made it easier to whittle them down. Steel mills were closed, the rubber tire industry crumbled under foreign competition, and the garment industry was almost wiped out by imports from developing countries. Many union contractors in construction either switched to nonunion work or set up nonunion subsidiaries, reducing the union share of construction from 80 to 33 percent in the course of 20 years.

Unions were forced to make concessions under employer threats to move their operations to nonunion areas within the country or overseas. Some employers engaged in bargaining tactics designed to bring about a strike, then ousted the union by hiring replacements. They were able to do this because American employers enjoy an advantage shared in few other industrial countries, the relative ease of finding strikebreakers. Bus drivers, machinists, coal miners, and other skilled workers could be secured despite the violence with which union pickets often greeted their arrival on the job.

Government policy favored employers determined to fight the unions. The National Labor Relations Board, originally set up to protect the right of workers to organize without employer interference, hindered organization by dilatory administrative practices. The Department of Labor, for many years the main point of contact between the federal government and the unions, became employer oriented.

Many American employers continue to engage in collective bargaining, and there are some who welcome union cooperation. But there is an attitude of hostility on the part of a substantial number of employers who operate nonunion and want to stay that way, and this tends to permeate the atmosphere of industrial relations. Widespread publicity given to defeats of striking unions does not help the union cause.

THE DEVELOPING COUNTRIES

Employer attitudes toward trade unions vary widely among developing countries. At one pole are the relatively few with well-established labor market institutions in which collective bargaining is routinely practiced. At the other pole, unions are barely tolerated and employers either ignore them or control them. To complicate matters, attitudes are subject to rapid change, depending on the policies of the government in power and their relations with it.

The transformation of Korean employer policies in best illustrated by events that occurred at the four largest enterprises during the 1980s.

Hyundai

The giant conglomerate operated nonunion until 1987. In that year, a local union established at one of its engine plants spread quickly to other auto plants and shipyards. The company countered by registering a company union with the appropriate government agency and declared a lockout against attempts to coordinate the new locals. After secret negotiations, the vice minister of Labor announced that Hyundai was prepared to negotiate at 8 of its 12 companies. Contracts were signed at 3, but for the rest the unions were declared by a government agency to have organized contrary to law, and their leaders were imprisoned. After much turmoil and violence, Hyundai was forced to recognize the union in additional plants, but insisted on its right to approve union officers. "The union at Hyundai is not likely to go away, but it is constantly subject to the interference of the company. . . . It will require years of consistent struggle before Hyundai will accept it as a legitimate partner."[15]

Samsung

The man who founded this 36-company enterprise, Lee Byung Chul, was quoted as saying, "I will have earth cover my eyes before a union is permitted at Samsung." The enterprise had an extensive program to instill loyalty to the company in the work force when unionism threatened and to register a company union before an outside organization could do so. Friends committees were established to counter the unions, splitting the employees. "The Samsung approach to unionism has been quite successful in imposing the old authoritarian structures. By adapting the policies of colonial Japan, Samsung is showing the way on how to beat unions even in the midst of a strong trend in the other direction."[16]

Daewoo

This conglomerate of 25 companies maintained a centralized non-union policy. It had its first skirmish with a union in 1985 and responded by dismissing the union leaders. The situation was complicated by the existence of a company-dominated organization. In 1987, in the midst of the general labor uprising, partisans of the new organization marched through the factory of Daewoo Motors, seized the president and vice president of the company, and forced them to bow down in front of the workers. This was followed in the ensuing days by riots and jailings. Similar disorders took place at the Daewoo Shipyards, where several workers immolated themselves. In the end, Daewoo signed agreements for these two companies, but the unions gained only a precarious foothold.

Goldstar

Consisting of 27 companies, Goldstar has had unions in its plants since the 1960s, although they were under company influence if not control. When the union wave began to roll in 1987, wage increases and decentralization of bargaining to the factory level kept things quiet. Two years later, however, strikes and demonstrations led to arbitration by a government agency, resulting eventually in a settlement. The unions here gained a greater degree of acceptance than at the three other corporations.

These events summarize the state of industrial relations in Korea since 1987. Unions have gained bargaining rights in a portion of industry but against strong employer opposition. The 1987 breakthrough, reminiscent of what happened in the United States in 1936–1937, enabled unions to achieve a substantial membership, attesting to the pent-up resentment over earlier authoritarian labor relations.

The case of Taiwan is somewhat similar to that of Korea but with less turmoil. The change in government policy in 1987, signaled by the lifting of martial law, enabled nascent unions to come out in the open and begin organizing. Employers resisted by discharging activists and setting up blacklists, but the unions continued to grow. While there are some employer associations, bargaining is carried on mainly at the level of the enterprise.

The country's largest firm, Formosa Plastics, made it clear that adversarial bargaining was not part of its plan for labor relations, a view that was shared by other firms. "The drive for independent labor unions lost momentum due to tougher tactics on the part of employers, as well as the slowing of the Taiwan economy. Even well-established unions have taken a cautious stance towards confrontation with employers and authorities."[17]

However, all was not quiet on the labor front. The number of labor disputes increased, some taking the form of wildcat strikes. Public policy began to favor collective bargaining, although it took hold slowly. In 1991, the Petroleum Workers Union threatened a strike at the Chinese Petroleum Corporation, despite a government warning against any stoppage of work, and managed to win an increase greater than the company's bonus offer. A number of collective agreements have been signed, but Taiwan's employers still do not relish doing business with trade unions and remain generally hostile to them.

Entrepreneurs are held in high regard in Korea and Taiwan. They have been the engines behind the phenomenal growth that lifted the two countries from Asian poverty to near developed-country standards in two decades. They have been ruthless in their quest for profits and have often given short shrift to employee complaints. Events after 1987 made it clear that the complaints could no longer be neglected. The best index of discontent is the rapid growth of unionism. Employers in Western countries faced the same problems a century ago, and it took some time for them to recognize that new forms of industrial relations were called for. It will probably be a while before similar adjustments are made in countries such as Korea and Taiwan. In the absence of political authoritarianism, industrialization brings unionization.

Malaysian employer associations are treated in the same manner as trade unions. They are required to register with the director-general of Trade Unions, and the members must be from the same industry or occupation. The central organization of private sector employers is the Malaysian Employers Federation (MEF). As of 1986, there were 19 employer associations, of which only 7 covered the entire country. The MEF had 750 individual companies as members, plus 4 of the national employer associations. It provides advice on how to answer trade union demands and provides assistance in collective bargaining, although it does not bargain on its own. It represents employers on tripartite bodies. However, individual employers are free to determine their own bargaining policies, and there is a good deal of variation among them.[18]

An example of the problems that the Malaysian unions have in securing recognition from their employers is provided by firms in the electronics industries. The Electrical Industry Workers' Union attempted to organize them in the 1970s, but the government registrar denied recognition by ruling that the firms were in the electronics industry, not the electrical industry. When the AFL-CIO filed a petition requesting that Malaysia's tariff privileges be suspended, the Ministry of Labor announced that only company unions would be permitted in electronics. In a test case involving the Harris Solid State Company, a company union sought recognition. "The campaign by the union . . . was long and bitter, with both management and union accusing each other of unfair tactics, and with both sides accusing the government of favoring the other. After the union demonstrated that a majority of Harris Solid State workers belonged to the union, the government ordered Harris to recognize the union."[19] The victory proved to be a Pyrrhic one; two of the three Harris subsidiaries in Malaysia were closed and the union members discharged.

Although collective bargaining is the norm in Malaysia, and while most employers abide by the legislation that gives workers the right to organize, recalcitrant employers can often resist effectively, because the government is concerned with protecting manufacturing firms. Strikes are rare and of short duration. More than half of the employees in the public sector are in company unions, which is the model preferred by the government for private employment as well. The Malaysian unions are still a long way from acquiring sufficient power to assert their legitimacy and equality in the bargaining process. Still, compared with the situation in most developing nations, the opposition of employers to unionization is relatively muted, and the unions are better off than their neighbors in Southeast Asia.

Labor relations in Thailand are considerably less institutionalized than in Malaysia, a result to which more recent industrialization, political instability, a fragmented labor movement, and the large state sector have contributed. At the national level, there is the Employers Confederation of Thailand (ECOT), which was formed in 1977 and numbers among its members 20 employer associations as well as individual employers. Collective bargaining in the private sector, where it exists, is at the enterprise level.

The travails of the labor movement under a succession of military governments have already been discussed. Employer attitudes have been summarized in the following terms:

Most establishments have no operational grievance procedures. Thai management is traditionally paternalistic, especially in small and medium sized firms. In the Thai firm, docility is more valued than ability, and obedience and loyalty more important than productivity. . . . Employers have grown sophisticated in combatting union activities. They employ lockouts against strikes, and are able to find legal reasons to fire key union personnel. . . . Industrial relations in Thailand are slowly becoming modern.[20]

Collective bargaining in the Philippines revived with the demise of the Marcos administration in 1986. The number of employees covered by collective agreements rose from 262,000 in 1986 to 535,000 in 1991. Employers are represented by the Employers' Confederation of the Philippines and affiliated industry associations.

A tripartite Industrial Peace Accord was reached in 1990 with the participation of the employer associations and all the unions except those under leftist control. It contained a vague commitment to democracy, free enterprise, and voluntary modes of settling labor disputes. To monitor its operation, a tripartite Industrial Peace Council was established. The government also promoted labor-management cooperation councils, and by the end of 1990, there were 255 at the plant level, 48 at regional levels, and 51 covering entire industries, with 50,000 workers participating in the various councils.

"Worker rights conditions in the goods producing sectors in the Philippines with U.S. investment tend to be better than those in the Philippine industry taken as a whole. Firms with U.S. investment are extensively organized by all of the unions within the broad spectrum — left to right — of local labor organizations. Nearly all of these firms have concluded collective bargaining agreements. The labor relations scene in these companies is at least as active (if not more so) as that in industry generally."[21] American employers seem to be less hostile to unions abroad than they are at home.

Philippine labor relations have settled down since the outburst that began in 1986. It would be an exaggeration, however, to say that there is widespread willingness of Philippine employers to bargain with unions. In 1990, total industrial employment was 14.6 million, while little more than 500,000 were covered by collective agreements. The Aquino administration, while not pro-union, did foster better industrial relations than had prevailed earlier. Unemployment and lagging development have been greater obstacles to union organization than recent employer attitudes.

The final Asian country to be considered is India. Collective bargaining prevails in the industrial sector, and union density is substantial in that sector. The central body of organized employers is the Council of Indian Employers (CIE), which has three major constituents: the All India Organization of Employers (AIOE), the Employers Federation of India (EFI), and the Standing Conference on Public Enterprises (SCOPE). Each in turn has both associated and individual members. As of 1986, 59 associations and 144 individual firms belonged to the AIOE; the EFI had 31 associations and 183 individual firms; and SCOPE had 215 combined.[22] Most member firms are large and relatively well disposed to enter into collective bargaining.

The functions of the employer groups vary considerably from one to another. A few have a long tradition of bargaining relationships, including the Ahmedabad Millowners Association, the Bombay Millowners Association, the Cement Manufacturers Association, and the Indian Banks Association. For the most part, however, they act in a consultative capacity, leaving bargaining to the individual firms. There is also a great deal of variation in employer attitudes. Some act in a paternalistic manner and expect their employees to be completely loyal to the firm. Younger and more dynamic managers may adopt more aggressive policies and deal with their unions only at arm's length. However, bolstered by government promotion, participation in collective bargaining is the prevailing ethic.

India is not a country without work stoppages, which may be long and bitter. "Harassment of trade union organizers is not new to India. In September, 1991, however, unknown assailants went beyond the usual bounds and killed . . . independent trade union leader Shankar Guha Niyogi. Niyogi had been involved in organizing tribal workers in the Chattisgarh region of the state and was known for his non-violent, unconventional approach to the problems of unorganized workers. Trade unionists charged that his assassination was engineered by antagonized local business men."[23] It is also interesting that more days of work are lost due to lockouts than to strikes. This is not entirely the result of employer aggressiveness, however, but may reflect employer efforts to shut down their plants without cumbersome and time-consuming bureaucratic requirements.

India's industrial relations system is not typical of those in developing countries. India has had many years of experience with manufacturing and with political democracy. Many problems that unions have with their employers result from the unions themselves. "While unions accuse the employers of causing interunion rivalry and generally manipulating the union dynamics at enterprise level, the employers voice their concern as the victims of the inability of trade unions in regard to the modus operandi for determining a bargaining agent. Employers argue that interunion rivalry has caused the greatest damage to industrial peace in the post-independence era."[24] As far as employer attitudes are concerned, the Indian unions have among the best conditions for successful organization in the developing world.

The four countries under review in Latin America are hardly in the same development category as those in Asia, at least with respect to labor relations. Independent for more than a century, they have been on a slow growth path, with frequent interludes of stagnation. Three have had periodic military coups. They are developing countries in the sense that their per capita GNP leads to their definition as lower-middle-income countries by the World Bank. On the other hand, all have had powerful trade unions at one time or another and are accustomed to collective bargaining. Their labor institutions are well developed if not stable.

Brazil was under military rule from 1964 to 1985. Until 1978, collective bargaining was minimal, with wages regulated by the government and disputes settled by labor courts. Collective bargaining was reintroduced in 1978, and beginning in 1982 factory committees were established to provide worker representation at the plant level. Unions gained more freedom of action when a civilian government came into office.

However, Brazil still remained under the influence of the so-called New State, modeled on the Italian fascist system and introduced by Getulio Vargas, who was president from 1937 to 1945 and again from 1950 to 1954. Under this scheme, the economy was divided into seven sectors, and labor and employer associations were formed in each. Financed by taxes on wages and payrolls, they dealt with one another under the close supervision of the Ministry of Labor.

When genuine collective bargaining became possible in 1985, the Vargas cult had not entirely disappeared:

At the heart of Vargas' system lay the concept of the state as intermediary, separating labor and management from direct contact with each other. Interest conflicts were to be resolved not through collective bargaining but paternalistically, by special labor courts. Given this context, Brazil's return to democracy in 1985 found neither labor nor business equipped to do that which in Western democracies is considered normal: deal directly with each other. Without experience, freedom to engage in collective bargaining did not lead routinely to contracts renewed through negotiation. Both labor and management had to acquire the prerequisite skills, then the habits, on the basis of which successful agreements could be crafted.[25]

There were widespread strikes during the first few years of freedom, directed more against government price stabilization measures than employers. In fact, some employers raised wages above government guidelines to preserve real wages against rampant price inflation. Efforts in 1990 to reach a national tripartite agreement to stabilize wages and prices failed.

Employer-employee relations during the 1980s were overshadowed by the limitations imposed by the military during the first half and by inflation during the second. The unions' problem was not so much with employers, who could raise wages and pass the higher cost to consumers, but with government policy that had the effect of reducing real wages.

The condition of the Chilean unions during the 1980s has already been related. There was some collective bargaining, but the unions were at a distinct disadvantage, particularly in the larger enterprises. Their leaders complained of management abuses, including surveillance, verbal abuse, and dismissal of union activists. There were some strikes, but their objectives were rarely achieved.[26]

The basic conditions for genuine collective bargaining were lacking. "The alleged equality of the parties at the bargaining table does not in fact exist once machinery has been introduced to favor the employers' representatives. The latter already have an advantage over the workers because of the considerable manpower reserves available (including skilled labor) and because the law permits mass dismissals at no further cost to the enterprise."[27] It was not until after the end of the decade that a return to pre-Pinochet collective bargaining and restraints on employers began to be effectuated.

Although Argentinian military rule ended in 1983, it was not until 1988 that conditions permitting collective bargaining were restored. This was due largely to the efforts of the Alfonsin administration to dislodge the Peronist leadership of the unions, an effort that failed. Until the military took over, the trade unions enjoyed considerable power, and collective bargaining was the order of the day.

Management was also well organized. Employer associations that had been suppressed were revitalized in 1983 and began dealing with the unions informally. As in the case of Brazil, inflation meant that it was the government rather than the employers that was responsible for the constraints on union demands. Consumer prices increased at an average annual rate of 328 percent from 1980 to 1990. Some employer associations negotiated wage increases in excess of government guidelines to allay worker unrest.

In 1990, with inflation under some control, the government began to allow private-sector wages to be determined by collective bargaining. The unions resumed their role in the bargaining process and regained their legitimacy.

Mexico is the only Latin American country reviewed here in which industrial relations maintained a steady pace throughout the 1980s, undisturbed by political change. Both union and employer groups kept their affiliations with the PRI, the dominant political party, and this served to temper employer attitudes toward the unions.

Inflation was not as virulent as elsewhere in Latin America, but it was nevertheless a major factor in labor relations. Consumer prices rose at an average annual rate of 73.8 percent from 1980 to 1990. Neither employers nor unions were happy with the wage-price controls imposed by the government, but they went along. Collective bargaining continued within the guidelines. Labor relations were not turbulent, but strikes were not uncommon, although they were not generally successful. Some were declared illegal for failure to follow statutory requirements, while others led to plant closures. Union rivalry was not uncommon as the cause of conflict.

Employers could and did oppose specific union demands, but they could not challenge their legitimacy and seek to destroy them. Unions were shielded by the corporatist structure of the PRI and particularly the dominant organization, the CTM, and its affiliates. It is fair to say that as far as employer attitudes were concerned, the Mexican unions shared with those of India a degree of recognition not often found in developing countries.

Employers in Kenya are organized in the Federation of Kenya Employers (FKE), which dates from 1959. "The FKE is widely considered to be the best run and most effective employers group in Africa. Numbering 2,325 members (up from little more than 200 at independence), it covers the entire spectrum of Kenya's employment scene. In addition to its traditional practice of representing its members in collective bargaining and before the Kenya Industrial Court, the FKE has expanded its activities to include management training programs."[28]

Wages are determined by collective bargaining, and while there are numerous strikes, they are mainly over local conditions — dismissals, working hours, bonuses, and separation pay. Collective agreements must be registered with the Ministry of Labor. One index of the stability of the system is the increase in the number registered, from 242 in 1982 to 384 in 1988.

Despite the decline of the Kenyan unions during the 1980s, their ability to bargain continued unabated. As one of the few African countries with a functioning labor relations system, Kenya and its unions have been the beneficiaries of assistance provided by outside agencies, including the International Labour Organization, the International Confederation of Free Trade Unions, the African-American Labor Center, the German Freidrich Ebert Foundation, the Finnish Development Agency, and the Israeli Labor Federation. This international spotlight has served to bolster the bargaining strength of the Kenyan unions.

Only about 5 percent of the Egyptian labor force is employed in the formal private sector. Some private firms keep the unions out by paying salaries and benefits that exceed those paid by the country's major employer, the government. Legislation of long standing confers a virtual guarantee of permanent employment on those employed in the public sector, a priceless benefit in a country of endemic underemployment. In 1970, the chairman of the Trade Union Federation became minister of Manpower and Vocational Training, a position he held simultaneously with his union office. He was replaced by the head of the Textile Workers Union in 1986. It is political influence rather than bargaining power that enables the Egyptian unions to offer resistance to private employers.

SUMMARY

This brief review of employer policies and attitudes in the 25 countries in the sample suggests that there are not many in which employers are so hostile to well-established unions that they seek to create union-free environments. In a few countries, they look upon unions as positive actors in industrial relations and maintain cordial relations with them. For the most part, employers are constrained by government policy or union power to engage in collective bargaining in a permanent fashion. In any event, except perhaps in developing countries in which employers contribute to the suppression of union activity, the decline in union density, where it has taken place, cannot be attributed to growing employer antipathy.

One interesting fact that emerges is that the organization of employers tends to improve relationships with unions. Employers do associate in order to present a stronger front in bargaining, but it is rare to find employer groups that were formed to destroy unions. Employer associations tend to provide professionalism in the conduct of industrial relations. Their function is to promote industrial peace rather than warfare.

NOTES

1. See Jonas Pontusson and Savosh Kuruvilla, "Swedish Wage Earner Funds: An Experiment in Economic Democracy," *Industrial and Labor Relations Review,* July 1992, p. 779.

2. Norman F. Dufty, "Employers Associations in Australia," in John T. Windmuller and Allan Gladstone, eds., *Employers Associations and Industrial Relations* (Oxford, England: Clarendon, 1984), p. 123.

3. Ronald F. Bunn, "Employer Associations in the Federal Republic of Germany," in Windmuller and Gladstone, eds., *Employers Associations,* p. 105, (by permission of the Oxford University Press).

4. Steven Tolliday and Jonathan Zeitlin, *The Power to Manage* (London: Routledge, 1991), p. 224.

5. Pradeep Kumar and Dennis Ryan (eds.), *Canadian Labor Movement in the 1980s* (Kingston, Ontario, Canada: Queen's University, 1988), p. 43.

6. Mark Thompson, "Canadian Industrial Relations," in Greg J. Bamber and Russel D. Lansbury, eds., *International and Comparative Industrial Relations* (London: Allen & Unwin, 1987), p. 80.

7. Roger G. McElrath, *Trade Unions and the Industrial Relations Climate in Spain* (Philadelphia: Wharton School, 1989), p. 175.

8. Jordi Estivill and Josep M. de la Hoz, "Transition and Crisis: The Complexity of Spanish Industrial Relations," in Guido Baglioni and Colin Crouch, eds., *European Industrial Relations* (London: Sage, 1990), p. 279.

9. E. G. A. Armstrong, "Employer Associations in Great Britain," in Windmuller and Gladstone, eds., *Employers Associations,* p. 54.

10. Readers who would like more information on this subject are urged to see a British film entitled *I'm All Right Jack,* in which the late Peter Sellers plays the role of a Marxist shop steward.

11. W. Grant and D. Marsh, *The CBI* (London: Holder and Stoughton, 1977), p. 80.

12. P. B. Beaumont, *Changes in Industrial Relations* (London: Routledge, 1990), p. 80.

13. Japan Institute of Labor, *Japan Labor Bulletin,* March 1992.

14. Japan Institute, *Japan Labor Bulletin,* July 1989.

15. George E. Ogle, *Korea: Dissent within the Economic Miracle* (London: Zed Books, 1990), p. 125.

16. Ogle, *Korea,* p. 129.

17. U.S. Department of Labor, *Foreign Labor Trends: Taiwan, 1990–1991,* p. 2.

18. Marilyn Avniceldin, *Malaysian Industrial Relations* (Singapore: McGraw-Hill, 1990), pp. 16–19.

19. U.S. Department of Labor, *Foreign Labor Trends: Malaysia, 1990–1991,* p. 11.

20. U.S. Department of Labor, *Foreign Labor Trends: Thailand, 1990–1991,* pp. 7–8.

21. U.S. Department of Labor, *Foreign Labor Trends: Philippines, 1988–1989,* p. 17.

22. C. S. Venkata Ratnam, *The Employers' Dilemma* (Bombay: Solar Foundation, 1989), pp. 18–26.

23. U.S. Department of Labor, *Foreign Labor Trends: India, 1990-1991*, p. 4.

24. Ratnam, *Employers' Dilemma*, p. 127.

25. U.S. Department of Labor, *Foreign Labor Trends: Brazil, 1989*, pp. 10-11.

26. Manuel Barrera, Helia Henriquez, and Tertesita Selame, *Trade Unions and the State in Present Day Chile* (Geneva: United Nations Research Institute for Social Development), pp. 65-68.

27. Barrera, Henriquez, and Selame, *Trade Unions*, p. 111.

28. U.S. Department of Labor, *Foreign Labor Trends: Kenya, 1987-1988*, p. 6.

CHAPTER 7

Public Opinion

This chapter reviews public opinion polls relating to trade unions, covering both members and nonmembers, for as many countries in the sample as turned up in a library search. Not surprising, most are for the industrial countries. Polls for developing countries are rare.

Many objections have been raised about the validity of polling for establishing attitudes in a meaningful way. Even if the sampling is done according to accepted statistical canons, there are other problems. Polls provide only a snapshot of opinion unless they are repeated over time. Opinions are subject to rapid change in the face of particular events—in the case of unions, major strikes. The wording of the poll can have significant effects on the results. Individuals may be reluctant to reveal their real views in as sensitive an area as unionism. Trade unions may be reluctant to supply membership lists, making it difficult to secure representative samples of union members.[1]

Notwithstanding these drawbacks, opinion polls can provide some help in tackling the question of union growth and decline. Has there been any change in the evaluation of the costs and benefits that individuals perceive as flowing from union membership? What attracts people to unions or keeps them away? Do the traditional goals of higher wages and shorter hours remain operative, or do different desires come to the fore? Direct questioning on these and similar matters may be of value as a supplement to the data that were considered in earlier chapters.

Trade Union Growth and Decline

Table 7.1
Public Views of Trade Unions (Percentage of Respondents)

	Canada [a]		United States [a]			United Kingdom [b]	
	Approve	Disapprove	Approve	Disapprove	Good	Bad
1970	54	30	59 (73)	26	60	24
1975	57	26	59 (78)	31	51	34
1980	54	30	55 (81)	35	60	29
1984	51	35	58 (85)	27	63 (83)	25
1985			59	30	67	22
1988			61	25	68	21
1989	56	33			68	24

Sources: Canada, Gary N. Chaison and Joseph B. Rose, *Continental Divide* (Hamilton, Ontario, Canada: McMaster University, 1988), *Index to International Public Opinion*, 1989–1990; United States, *1988 Gallup Survey of Public Opinion about Labor Unions;* United Kingdom, *Index to International Public Opinion*, 1984–1985, 1990.

Note: The numbers in parentheses indicate years. The difference between 100 percent and the totals for approval and disapproval represent replies of "don't know."

[a]The Canadian and U.S. polls asked: "In general, do you approve or disapprove of labor unions?"

[b]The U.K. poll asked: "For Great Britain as a whole, are unions good or bad?"

GENERAL PUBLIC ATTITUDES TOWARD UNIONS

One of the few internationally comparable time series available appears in Table 7.1. It contains relevant data for Canada, the United States, and Britain for the years 1970 to 1989. When asked whether they approved or disapproved of unions, a majority of Canadians expressed approval, although there was some sag in the approval rate in the mid-1980s, followed by recovery at the end of the decade. In the United States, there was a long slide in the approval rate from 76 percent in 1967 (not shown in Table 7.1) to a low point in 1981, with a substantial recovery by the end of the decade. As for Britain, the approval percentage rose steadily after 1975.

The British public appears to have expressed a considerably greater degree of confidence in the positive role of unions than was true in Canada and the United States, despite the anti-union line of the Thatcher government. And the U.S. unions had greater public support than their Canadian counterparts, despite the policies of the Reagan administration. Indeed, public disapproval seems to have been higher in Canada than in the United States or Britain, an interesting finding in view of the lesser degree of pro-employer bias on the part of the Canadian government. Nothing in these data suggests a relationship between union density and public approval.

Data for other countries are scattered. When the French public was asked in 1983, "What would you say the trade unions' effect was on the country in general?" the replies were:[2]

Constructive	28 percent
Negative	36
Neither	22
Undecided	14

Polled in 1989 on how useful unions were, 25 percent of French respondents found them very useful, 38 percent somewhat useful, 19 percent not very useful, 14 percent not at all useful, and 4 percent had no opinion.[3] However, this relatively positive response was somewhat offset by another poll relating to the degree of union influence:[4]

Too much	35 percent
Not enough	29
Just enough	28
No opinion	8

In general, despite the weakness of the French unions, they did seem to enjoy a relatively favorable public opinion.

The German public, asked in 1984 about its satisfaction with the way in which unions represented the interests of workers, replied:[5]

Very satisfied	2 percent
Mainly satisfied	20
Mainly dissatisfied	33
Very dissatisfied	20
Don't know	25

This was hardly a ringing endorsement of the unions in a country in which they are very strong.

Nor do the Italians appear to be enamored of their unions. When asked about union power in 1979, they answered:[6]

Very little power	13.9 percent
Too much power	45.2
About right	18.7
No opinion	22.3

The Swedish public, on the other hand, appeared to be satisfied with the status quo of union power in the same year:[7]

Too much power	29 percent
Too little power	18
Right amount	42
Don't know	11

A few polls are available for the developing countries. The least favorable is one for Argentina, where in 1983, 57 percent of the general public considered unions negative social institutions and 58 percent branded strikes as prejudicial to the interests of the nation. The reaction reflected the political hue of the unions. Among Peronists, 55 percent thought that unions "helped the situation" of the workers and 60 percent had a positive attitude toward strikes.[8]

In a 1986 choice between unions and managers in Argentina, the unions won a clear victory:[9]

	Unions	Managers
Total confidence	15 percent	7 percent
Quite a lot of confidence	28	15
Little confidence	33	41
No confidence	12	25
Don't know	11	12

Finally, while those in the Indian public who had some knowledge of unions held a generally favorable view of them in 1982, a large proportion appeared to be ignorant of union operations. When asked, "Do you think trade unions by and large protect the interests of their workers to a large extent, to some extent, not at all?" the replies were:[10]

	Large	Some	Not at all	Don't know
Total	8	32	15	45
Male	10	41	20	29
Female	5	17	8	70
Urban	8	33	19	40
Rural	7	32	12	49

It is difficult to read any connection between these results and trends in union density. However, the polls do suggest that during the 1980s, trade unions did not enjoy strong support among the general public in any of the countries for which data were available, with the exception of Sweden.

WHY JOIN (OR NOT JOIN) A UNION

Of greater relevance to this inquiry are the reasons given by individuals for joining or not joining unions. Despite the cautions stated previously, they begin to clarify the causes of trends in union density.

Table 7.2 shows an Australian poll vintage 1988. About 30 percent of those questioned were current trade unions members, while one-half had been members at some time. The questions were based on a scale of 1 to 5 with respect to union effectiveness in achieving specified objectives. About one-quarter of the respondents believed that unions were doing a poor job in obtaining higher wages against one-third who perceived a good job, not an overwhelming recommendation for what are generally regarded as a union's most important services. The unions received good grades for obtaining better fringe benefits, for improving health and safety on the job, and for handling grievances. They did not perform well in giving workers a voice in how they perform their jobs, in giving members a say in running the union, in telling members what the union is doing, or in providing suggestions about running the enterprise. On a key issue, improving job security, good union performance had a slight lead over poor performance.

A commentary on the results pointed out that union leaders were not regarded as democratic. As for the areas in which the unions scored well,

The ACTU [union] leadership has been very vocal over the period of the Accord [between the federal government and the ACTU] in its support, particularly for the centralized wage fixing system. The linkage between the very

Table 7.2
Community Attitudes of Australian Trade Union Activities

ITEMS	Poor job 1	2	3	4	Good job 5
Obtaining higher wages	9.8	13.0	41.9	23.6	11.6
Getting workers a say in how they do their jobs	13.8	18.2	43.1	19.0	5.8
Obtaining better fringe benefits	8.2	15.1	43.4	21.9	11.4
Improving job security	13.6	17.2	32.9	25.3	11.0
Giving members a say in how the union is run	30.5	23.9	24.9	13.9	6.8
Improving health and safety conditions on the job	5.6	7.2	25.7	37.8	23.7
Telling members what the union is doing	19.1	23.7	29.5	17.9	9.8
Handling workers complaints and grievances	12.2	12.9	39.4	23.1	12.4
Getting workers a say in how their employer runs the business	19.6	21.2	41.3	13.4	4.4

Source: Lawson K. Savery and Geoffrey N. Soutar, *Trade Union Effectiveness,* Western Australian Labor Market Research Center, 1990.
Note: Due to rounding, figures may not add up to 100 percent.

public support by the ACTU leaders for the Accord and subsequent pay rises and the new Occupational Health and Safety Acts could well have led the public to perceive that trade unions are doing a good job in the area of items covered by legislation, particularly in a Labor governed state such as Western Australia.[11]

Table 7.3
Canadian Polls: "Here are some of the things unions try to do for their members. Which is most important at the present time?" (Percentages of Replies)

	1958	1976	1981	1985
Security of employment	47	45	50	52
Better working conditions	11	19	19	18
Higher wages	7	11	10	7
Better pension plans	12	8	8	8
Profit sharing	8	7	9	5
Shorter working hours	4	3	1	3
Other	1	2	–	1
Can't say	8	6	4	6

Source: International Index of Public Opinion, 1984–1985, p. 274.

The results of an interesting Canadian poll appear in Table 7.3. Employment security won hands down as a desirable union objective, with better working conditions a distant second. The traditional union wage-and-hour functions hardly figured at all, nor did better pension plans and profit sharing score well.

A fairly recent British poll (Table 7.4) again puts employment security at the top of the preferred union agenda, although wages and working conditions rate higher than in Australia. The major disadvantage of belonging to a union was the necessity of abiding by union policy, with the closed shop and strikes next.

A U.S. survey of 1,029 men and women 18 years of age and older was conducted in 1988 (Table 7.5). The participants were asked whether union or nonunion employees were better off with respect to various working conditions. The unions scored well on wages, job security, and health insurance. They did not do as well on such less tangible items as advancement and promotion opportunities, recognition for good work, control of how work is done, and workplace privacy. That wage services rate higher in the United States than in Britain or Canada may be because union-nonunion wage differentials are better known in the United States.

Table 7.4
United Kingdom Poll on Attitudes toward Trade Unions, 1988 (Percentages of Replies)

" What do you think are the advantages of belonging to a trade union?"

Better wages	20
Better working conditions	25
Common front against employer	16
Official arbitration	4
Individual complaints dealt with	6
Job protection, legal representation	41
No advantage	14
Other	11

" What do you think are the disadvantages of belonging to a union?"

Have to follow union policy	26
Restrictive practices	6
Closed shop	11
Dues	3
Too political	4
Too many strikes	11
Too dominant	8
Other	7
No disadvantages	26
Don't know	17

Source: Index to International Public Opinion, 1988–1989, p. 214

A 1987 poll covered young people aged 15 to 24 in the European Common Market countries. Seventy-nine percent who were not union members explained why not:[12]

No union where I work 34 percent

Unions do not look after the interests

of people like me 5

My employer doesn't like unions 5

I don't believe in unions 26

I will join, but haven't yet 7

Other and no reply 23

Table 7.5
Comparison of Union and Nonunion Employees: United States, 1988

	Among Total Sample					
	Better Off %	Worse Off %	No Difference %	Can't Say %	Total %	No. of Int.
Wages and benefits (other than health insurance)	72	4	17	7	100	(1029)
Job security	65	5	23	7	100	(1029)
Health insurance	63	4	26	7	100	(1029)
Health and safety conditions	60	3	30	7	100	(1029)
Fair and consistent administration of policy by managers	47	8	34	11	100	(1029)
Discrimination on the basis of sex, race, age or handicap	45	6	40	9	100	(1029)
Control of the way in which work is performed	41	11	37	11	100	(1029)
Advancement or promotion opportunities	40	11	39	10	100	(1029)
Sexual harassment	35	6	46	13	100	(1029)
Recognition for work well done	27	13	50	10	100	(1029)
Privacy in the workplace	27	10	50	13	100	(1029)

Source: The Gallup Organization, *1988 Gallup Survey of Public Opinion about Labor Issues.*

Table 7.6
Reasons Given by Nonunionists in Norway for Not Joining Unions, 1988
(Percentage of Total)

	Men	Women
Work part time	3	18
No union that suits me	24	17
No union at my place of work	20	14
Dues are too high	1	3
Never been asked to join	7	11
I receive the union rate nonetheless	2	4
I oppose unions in principle	16	7
Other reasons	27	26

Source: Arvid Fennefoss, *Wage Earner Organization,* FAFO Report No. 081, Oslo: FAFO, 1988, p. 220.

The special circumstances of the Scandinavian countries, with their high union densities, give the reasons for not joining a union particular interest. In the Norwegian replies, shown in Table 7.6, those who did not join because there was no union at their place of work were presumably employed at small enterprises. A surprising number found no suitable union where they worked, while some of those who opposed unions in principle may have done so for religious reasons. The same sample of individuals was queried about desirable union priorities, and the replies (Table 7.7) suggest that the traditional union services of wages, working conditions, employment, and hours predominate. Recall that a system of codetermination exists in Norway, which may account for the absence of participation in enterprise decision making as a union priority.

QUALITY OF UNION SERVICES

Part of the problem faced by unions in attracting members may lie in the manner in which they conduct their affairs. Do prospective enrollees perceive that union leaders are concerned primarily with member interests, or do they have other objectives? Is union business conducted democratically? Have unions become too bureaucratic?

Table 7.7
What Trade Union Priorities Should Be, Norway, 1988 (Total Replies)

	Union		Nonunion	
	Men	Women	Men	Women
Wage questions	65	62	51	43
Conditions at work	45	48	48	40
Employment	35	26	38	33
Hours of work	34	39	23	21
Skill matters	24	17	17	13
Pensions	22	17	15	9
Equality	10	15	16	30
Young workers	13	7	14	19
Equalizing income	10	15	11	15
Solidarity with other workers	9	9	9	8
Possibility of obtaining loans	7	5	5	7
Cooperation with political parties	6	5	2	3

Source: Arvid Fennefoss, *Wage Earner Organization,* FAFO Report No. 081, Oslo: FAFO, 1988, p. 2127.

Workers in Australia and New Zealand are not enthusiastic about the effectiveness of unions in securing economic gains, strengthening workers' voice, or raising productivity, if the polls in Table 7.8 are to be believed. Only a minority of workers felt that the unions were doing a good job in obtaining economic gains. They were rated even lower, particularly in Australia, in providing an outlet for worker views. Only about one-quarter of the respondents thought that unions were handling grievances well, and even fewer believed that they had a say in how the unions were run. On the other hand, few felt that unions affected productivity negatively, and a substantial majority in both countries favored greater union-management cooperation. But there was no vote of confidence in union leadership at either the workplace or official levels, and there was a strong desire to conduct negotiations at the workplace. All in all, the quality of union services in Australia and New Zealand was not rated high.

Table 7.8
Poll on Effects of Unions, Australian and New Zealand Employees, 1988
(Percentage of Respondents)

	Australia	New Zealand
Union Provides Economic Gains (percent responding good or very good)		
Higher wages	31.0	24.4
Better fringe benefits	22.7	12.8
Improve job security	39.8	27.1
Improve health and safety	50.0	35.5
Union Provides Workers Voice (percent responding good or very good)		
Getting workers say in doing jobs	22.8	18.1
Giving members say in running union	20.9	24.2
Giving workers say in running business	14.9	16.4
Telling members what union is doing	14.3	23.6
Handling complaints and grievances	20.8	28.8
Unions Harm Productivity (percent who agree or agree strongly)		
Productivity greater without unions	15.7	14.3
Prefer negotiations at workplace level	67.4	60.0
Choice of union representative adequate	17.9	19.4
Desire for union -mgt. cooperation	60.2	58.2
Workplace union reps. should have more influence	31.0	36.6
Union officials should have more influence	30.0	30.0

Source: The BCA/NILS Industrial Relations Study, National Institute of Labor Studies, Working Paper Series No. 100, September 1988.

French citizens who were asked whether they trusted trade unions to defend their interests responded as follows in 1989:[13]

	All French	Wage Earners
Complete confidence	6 percent	7 percent
Some confidence	34	40
Little confidence	22	22
No confidence whatsoever	29	26
No opinion	9	5

The fact that 48 percent of French wage earners expressed little or no confidence in unions may help explain why union density is so low. However, German trade union members responded in somewhat the same vein in a country in which the unions have done well (1984):[14]

Very satisfied	5 percent
Mainly satisfied	40
Mainly dissatisfied	34
Very dissatisfied	11
Don't know	10

Of those who were dissatisfied, 26 percent believed that the unions represented the interests of functionaries rather than of members, 20 percent considered union demands to be unrealistic, 14 percent were opposed to a current union demand for a 35-hour week, and 12 percent were against strikes.

Unions were less highly regarded in Italy, where a majority of employees felt that their interests were being represented in only a slightly satisfactory manner (1986):[15]

	All Employees	Wage Earners
Highly satisfactory	2.9 percent	3.9 percent
Sufficiently satisfactory	27.7	31.5
Slightly satisfactory	50.0	50.9
Unsatisfactory	19.1	13.9

When Japanese employees were asked about the sources of their dissatisfaction at work, wages led the list, followed by hours of work and interpersonal relations. But this is how they would have resolved their problems in 1987:[16]

Complain to management	8 percent
Consult supervisors at work	20
Consult with fellow employees	31
Consult with union	8
Would do nothing in particular	30
Other	3

To the question of the level of unionism that most interested them, Japanese workers replied:

The enterprise level union	12
National unions'	15
Central federations	9
No interest	57
No answer	7

If these results are in any way reflective of Japanese employee attitudes, they show little enthusiasm with the Japanese system of enterprise-level unionism.

British polling data for 1980 and 1990, shown in Table 7.9, cast an interesting light on the evolution of public views on trade unions during the Thatcher years. There was a sharp drop in the percentage of respondents who thought that unions were too powerful, as well as in the belief that unions were controlled by extremists – although half were still of that view in 1990. More people thought that unions were essential in the protection of workers' interests, and there was an increase in the proportion who placed the blame for the poor performance of the British economy on management rather than unions.

There are some fragmentary British data less flattering to the unions. In 1990, 51 percent of a sample of the British public said that union leaders did not represent the views of ordinary members, while only 29 percent thought they did.[17] In 1985, 52 percent agreed with the proposition that union leaders were out of touch with their members while 23 percent disagreed; 69 percent said that one purpose of unionism was to gain power and money for the leadership. In the same poll, however, 76 percent agreed that unions improved wages, working condi-

Table 7.9
Public Opinion Poll on Trade Unions, Great Britain, 1980 and 1990 (Percentage of Total)

	1980			1990		
	Agree	Disagree	No opinion	Agree	Disagree	No opinion
Unions have too much power in Britain today	72	19	9	38	45	17
Most unions controlled by extremists and militants	70	20	10	50	30	20
Unions essential to protect workers' interests	72	16	12	80	11	9
Bad mgt. is more to blame than unions for British economic problems today	43	31	26	58	16	26

Source: Index to International Public Opinion, 1990–1991, p. 263.

tions, and job security, and 68 percent thought that unions ensure fair treatment for their members.[18] The British polls do not support the proposition that public dissatisfaction with union goals or operation is a major cause of their decline, although it has been suggested that political adversity increased union popularity and that the decline in strikes and inflation contributed to a favorable public opinion, if not to an increase in membership.[19]

For the United States, the 1985 polling data shown in Table 7.10 suggest that there was a strong belief in the right of workers to organize. Respondents split equally on the proposition that unions are not concerned with the welfare of the companies with which they bargain,

Table 7.10
Public Attitudes toward Trade Unions, United States, 1985 (Percentage of Total)

	Agree	Disagree	Can't Say
Unions good for the nation as a whole	69	26	5
Without union effort, most laws benefiting employees would be seriously weakened or repealed	68	21	11
Existing U.S. laws should be strengthened to prevent corp. from denying workers' right to organize	66	25	9
Unions have been too weak to protect their members	52	39	9
Most unions are not concerned about welfare of company with which they bargain	46	46	8
A union establishment is more likely to go out of business than a nonunion establishment	35	51	14

Source: The Gallup Poll, May 19, 1985.

while a majority of respondents believed that union firms were less likely to go out of business than nonunion firms.

Swedish evaluations of industrial democracy were mixed. Asked whether the steering committees of national unions and the top officials of LO were guilty of bossism, 59 percent said yes and 41 percent no. Fifty-five percent agreed with the statement that union representatives were too influential compared with ordinary members. Seventy percent said that local committees handled issues in a way that inspired confidence. Seventy-four percent were critical of various aspects of union elections; most frequently cited were too few candidates, too little variation in platforms, too frequent reelection of officers, and the underrepresentation of some groups. Only 35 percent thought that unions neglected important questions.[20] None of these criticisms has impaired the strength of the Swedish unions.

One additional issue worthy of note is the attitude of the general public and union members toward union affiliation with political parties. Half the Italian public believed that unions should be independent of political parties, while only 11 percent favored continuation of the situation in which unions are divided along political lines.[21] Some 55 percent of the Spanish public agreed on the need for union independence, although 33 percent, while favoring independence, thought that unions should occasionally enter into political accords on concrete issues.[22] In Sweden, where collective affiliation of LO with the Social Democratic party is of long standing, a surprising 64 percent of union members agreed that the relationship was undesirable, although some may have been members of non–LO federations.[23] In Great Britain, where the Labour party was originally established by the union movement, half of those questioned in an opinion poll felt that the unions had too much influence on the party, 8 percent not enough, while the rest said it was the right amount.[24]

SUMMARY

Public opinion polls revealed a generally supportive attitude toward the proposition that unions in Canada, Britain, and the United States played positive economic roles during the 1980s. The sharp density drops in the latter two countries were not accompanied by a decline in public favor. Swedish public opinion was pro-union, but in France, Germany, and Italy, unions were not overly popular. Unions were rated high in Brazil and India and low in Argentina. The data do not reveal any consistent relationship between general public attitudes and union density.

An interesting finding was that in several countries, views of both members and nonmembers about desirable union priorities did not rank the traditional objectives of wages and shorter working hours high. In Canada and Britain, employment security took first place, followed in Canada by working conditions and in Britain by wages and working conditions. Wages scored well in the United States, with job security and health insurance next. There is some indication of a shift of interest toward the desirability of a greater union effort in the enhancement of employment security. Hours of work received little mention.

How good a job are unions doing? Are they run democratically? In Australia, France, and Italy, the answer is "not too good" on the whole, while there is an even division of opinion in Germany. One of the most interesting findings was the lack of interest in enterprise unions among Japanese workers. As for democracy and union leadership, the mood seems to be lukewarm.

There appears to be some antipathy toward close union affiliation with political parties where this is the practice.

NOTES

1. For a discussion of these problems, see Martin Roiser and Tim Little, "Public Opinion, Trade Unions and Industrial Relations," *Journal of Occupational Psychology* 59 (1986): 259.
2. *Index to International Public Opinion,* 1982–1983, p. 271.
3. *Index to International Public Opinion,* 1989–1990, p. 246.
4. U.S. Department of Labor, *Foreign Labor Trends: France, 1989–1990,* p. 11.
5. *Index to International Public Opinion,* 1984–1985, p. 274.
6. *International Gallup Polls,* 1979, p. 121.
7. *Index to International Public Opinion,* 1979–1980, p. 318.
8. U.S. Department of Labor, *Foreign Labor Trends: Argentina, 1983,* pp. 13–14.
9. *Index to International Public Opinion,* 1986–1987, p. 337.
10. *Index to International Public Opinion,* 1982–1983, p. 275.
11. Lawson K. Savery and Geoffrey N. Soutar, *Trade Union Effectiveness,* Western Australian Labor Market Research Center, 1990, p. 17.
12. Commission of the European Communities, *Young Europeans in 1987* (Brussels: Commission of the European Communities, 1989), pp. 190–192.
13. U.S. Department of Labor, *Foreign Labor Trends: France, 1989–1990,* p. 11.
14. *Index to International Public Opinion,* 1984–1985, p. 234.
15. Gabriel Calvi, *Indagine sociale Italiana* (Milan: Franco Angele, 1987), p. 136.
16. *Index to International Public Opinion,* 1987–1988, p. 227.
17. *Index to International Public Opinion,* 1990–1991, p. 263.
18. *Index to International Public Opinion,* 1985–1986, p. 263.
19. P. K. Edwards and George Sayers Bain, "Why Are Trade Unions Becoming More Popular? Unions and Public Opinion in Britain," *British Journal of Industrial Relations,* November 1988, p. 311.
20. Leif Lewin, *Governing Trade Unions in Sweden* (Cambridge, Mass.: Harvard University Press, 1980), pp. 88, 89, 92, 103.
21. *International Gallup Polls* (Princeton, N.J.: Gallup, 1979), p. 121.
22. Sagardoy Bengoccha and David Leon Blanco, *El Poder Sindical en Espana,* 1982, p. 71.
23. Lewin, *Governing Trade Unions,* p. 86.
24. *Index to International Public Opinion,* 1990–1991, p. 263.

CHAPTER 8

Can Union Decline Be Arrested?

There is substantial literature on the reasons for union decline in the industrial nations, although little on the advance of unions in newly industrialized countries. Much of it is econometric in character, and most of the explanations are plausible. The problem is that the relevant causal factors are specific to individual countries; what works in one does not work in another.[1]

Some of the studies have been cited previously, but a brief sample of the literature may serve to illustrate this observation. An analysis of the U.S. experience led to the conclusion that union decline during the 1980s is largely accounted for by employer resistance to unionization plus an increase in the satisfaction of nonunion workers with their jobs and a decline in their belief that unionization would improve their wages and working conditions.[2] Management opposition to union organization is the principal factor cited in another study.[3]

In the case of Great Britain, among the explanatory factors for the decline in union density cited in a recent study were the business cycle, unemployment, a reduction in the number of large enterprises, and the shift in employment from manufacturing to services.[4] Another explanation was that "the vast bulk of the observed 1980s decline in union density in the U.K. is due to the changed legal environment for industrial relations."[5] While conceding that Conservative government legislation may have been a powerful force, a third study concluded that the growth of temporary and part-time work and the decline of the manufacturing sector were more fundamental.[6] Still another analysis finds fault with most of these explanations for insufficiently rigorous statistical methodology and comes down on the side of a particular macroeconomic model.[7]

France has had a socialist president since 1981, and government policy clearly did not contribute to undermining the unions. Indeed, legislation that was enacted favored the unions. Cited instead as underlying causes of union decline were the lack of meaningful wage bargaining, heavy unemployment, the shift from manufacturing to services, and the ideological split in the labor movement.[8] At least the first and last of these factors would not apply to the United States and Britain.

In Australia, where a Labor government was in power during the 1980s, half of union decline was attributed to structural shifts in employment, supplemented by such additional factors as a reduction in the size of firms, a change in public sentiment against unions, adverse legislation at the level of the individual states, management strategies, and a dislike of union participation in government wage-restraint policies.[9] A study of the union situation in Alberta, a province in Canada, advanced the argument that the factors at work were the shrinkage of manufacturing employment, the failure of the unions to adapt their traditional service agendas to a new economic environment, and the domination of the provincial government by the Conservatives.[10]

The problem of union decline has been attacked from a psychological point of view, delineating three theoretical approaches: frustration-aggression theory, rational choice theories, and interactional theory. A wide range of studies is slotted into one or another of these categories, with some interesting observations.[11] Another survey of the relevant psychological literature focuses on the choice by an individual employee whether to support unionization and finds this material highly informative. "There is a pretty well agreed upon set of variables that can be utilized. We suggest that there is also some useful theory available."[12]

It is quite likely that many factors cited in what is now a voluminous literature did indeed contribute to union decline in individual countries. One need only look at the tremendous shrinkage of large-scale heavy industry in the United States or the migration of labor-intensive industries to Asia to appreciate that structural change has been a potent factor. A pro-employer government is not a recipe for union prosperity. Unemployment tends to bring about a serious drain on union membership and finances.

There are very few exceptions to the decline of unions in the industrialized nations. The Scandinavian unions fared better for reasons that are considered later. Most of the rest followed the general pattern. Austria, The Netherlands, Portugal, and Switzerland experienced double-digit percentage union declines during the 1980s. Belgium is a mixed case: When measured by recorded membership, density rose by 2.4 percent from 1980 to 1988, but when measured by employed membership, it fell by 6.2 percent. The difficulty is to explain why the various factors, which differed in considerable degree from country to country, converged in the 1980s to produce for the first time in modern history the general debilitation of a social institution that appeared to be healthy and vigorous not many years ago. Unions have risen and fallen in the past but not all together. Are there some fundamental forces at work to help explain this unique phenomenon?

By way of a footnote: The task of assembling data for the developing countries was undertaken for comparative purposes. In 5 of the 12 countries covered, union density actually increased during the 1980s, and 3 of the others witnessed only moderate declines. The term *general decline* applies only to the countries with mature economies in which unionism is of long standing.

WHY WERE UNIONS FORMED?

Unions were a reaction to the hardships imposed upon working people by the process of industrialization. The change from agrarian to industrial societies uprooted people from their traditional homes and work. The more rapid the course of industrialization, the more radical the response was. Where the machine replaced the artisan at a relatively slow pace, where people had more time to adjust, the unions they formed tended to be moderate in character. Where there was a rapid rise of manufacturing, more radical ideologies tended to prevail.

Great Britain, where the Industrial Revolution began, was also the first country to see the birth of a labor movement. The United States was not far behind, and as industry spread to continental Europe, so did unionism. While there were unions in some developing countries even when they were under colonial domination, particularly in transportation, it was not until several decades after World War II that labor organization became more widespread. The years since 1970 have seen a virtual explosion of unionism in the newly industrialized countries that achieved high rates of economic growth.

The agendas of the new unions were concerned mainly with the obvious needs of their members. High on the list of demands was improvement in the level of compensation. One of the first national unions established in the United States, the Typographical Union, at its 1853 convention listed "a just remuneration for labor" as its principal objective. In Britain, "1853 was a key year for the Lancashire and Cheshire cotton industry. Prices were going up, industry was prosperous, and demands for higher wages were made in almost every town."[13] Indeed, higher wages were a necessity if unions were to survive, because workers living at the margin of existence could not provide adequate financial support for them.

Reducing hours of work was a second major objective. The genesis of the Labor Day holiday in the United States was a parade in New York City in 1884 held to promote adoption of an eight-hour day. Samuel Gompers wrote, "We want eight hours, we are determined to have eight hours, we shall try to aid those who are in a condition by May 1, 1890, to obtain eight hours and hope to obtain their assistance in return at some future time."[14] In Britain, the Nine Hours League was established in the early 1970s by the Amalgamated Engineers, supported by the Northumberland miners, and succeeded in reaching this goal after a strike. The eight-hour day was a prime objective all over Europe, and it remains one in the developing world today.

These were the most important agenda items for the early unions but not the only ones. Improvement of safety and health conditions on the job was a perpetual quest. The coal mining unions in particular were committed to improving mine safety, and the British National Miners' Association succeeded in getting legislation through Parliament as early as 1860.

An affiliate of the First International, in urging the formation of trade unions in Germany in 1868, resolved that "whereas experience teaches that sickness, invalidity, and old age can best be cared for by the trade unions, the convention directs the members and especially the executive committee to put their best efforts into the formation of nationally organized trade unions."[15] This was based upon earlier British experience with so-called friendly societies that paid benefits to cover these contingencies, as did the pioneering U.S. unions. Current unemployment compensation systems were based on trade union unemployment funds in many European countries. These were initially financed by the members themselves, followed by government subsidies, and eventually transformed into full-fledged government schemes.

Not least among labor's objectives was a mechanism providing for dignity in the employment relationship. This meant not only collective bargaining but also the establishment of grievance machinery that would enable a worker to secure redress for unfair treatment by management. Without a union, the worker had to depend on the employer's largesse, which was not always forthcoming.

Unions also endeavored to secure through political action what they could not get directly. The Knights of Labor, a predecessor of the American Federation of Labor (AF of L), pledged to work for the enactment of a weekly pay law, a mechanics' lien law, prevention of child labor, prohibiting the leasing out of convict labor, and equal pay for women. Free public education was a major union objective where it did not already exist. To attain these goals, unions entered into partnership with socialist parties. In some countries, as in Britain, they took the initiative in founding closely allied political parties and contributed to their support in the expectation that there would be commensurate returns.

It was the key ideas of mutual protection and benefit that motivated working people to form unions. They hoped to gain protection from arbitrary management acts and to benefit from higher wages, shorter hours, and improved working conditions. If an individual had been asked during the first century of modern unionism why he or she was joining a union, it would have been easy to reply. There were setbacks in various countries occasioned by particular events—depression, war, political upheavals—but the trend of membership sloped upward. When the Labour party defeated Winston Churchill in 1945, and when the U.S. labor movement played a leading role in the election of President Truman in 1948, when the trade unions of Germany, Italy, and Japan recruited millions of workers within five years of the end of hostilities, it would have been difficult to predict anything but a bright future for unionism.

ARE UNIONS STILL NEEDED?

What went wrong? Why did decline set in so soon after unions had reached the peak of their power and influence? For some countries, the turning point—when the density trend began to move down—came quickly. The United States came first, in 1962, followed by Japan in 1970 and France in 1975. The turning point was reached for four countries between 1978 and 1980—Britain, Italy, Germany, and New Zealand. In Canada, density continued to rise until 1983 and in Australia until 1985.

What appears to have happened was that the unions were the victims of their own success. The rise of the welfare state—the expansion of government programs and services—reduced the appeal of unionism by generalizing the benefits that had attracted employees in the past. When potential members began to weigh the costs of joining unions against the anticipated benefits, they began to stay out.

A welfare state can be defined as one in which a substantial proportion of the national product is redistributed by the government in the form of income—positive benefits. The data in Table 8.1 indicate that by 1986, all the industrial nations in the sample could be described as welfare states. During the 16-year period of 1970 to 1986, a substantial increase in most social security expenditures took place. Pensions and health received the lion's share.

Wages

Unions are still able to produce higher wages even where their power has diminished. In the United States, for example, it has been estimated that the union-nonunion wage differential is on the order of 10 to 20 percent, varying with age, education, seniority, and economic condi-

Table 8.1
Social Security Expenditures, 1970 and 1986

	Social security benefits as a % of GDP		Allocation of expenditures, 1986, percent of total					
	1970	1986	Sickness	Work Injuries	Pensions	Unemployment	Family Allowances
Australia	10.9	9.1	16.3	4.5	53.4	17.0	8.7
Canada	13.2	15.6	48.2	4.1	27.8	10.2	9.7
Denmark	14.5	25.5	31.5	1.6	42.4	22.4	2.2
France	13.9	27.2	31.2	–	44.1	10.0	14.8
Germany	23.1[a]	22.7	32.3	3.0	50.1	10.8	3.8
Italy	10.0[b]	10.0	3.7	–	88.5	3.6	4.3
Japan	4.8	11.5	47.2	3.1	44.8	4.3	0.6
N. Zealand	9.9	17.4	31.4	4.0	55.2	5.3	4.0
Norway	14.8	29.5	46.8	3.1	42.5	2.0	5.6
Spain	15.3[a]	17.2	25.6	3.4	51.1	18.5	1.3
Sweden	18.2	30.1	34.8	0.9	48.1	6.7	15.5
UK	12.8	19.4	38.6	1.1	46.0	9.3	10.1
US	11.8[a]	12.0	17.0	6.3	69.5	7.2	–

Source: International Labour Office, *The Cost of Social Security* (Geneva: ILO, 1986).
[a]1980
[b]1984

tions. The differential may be accompanied by the willingness of unions to tolerate unemployment rather than make wage concessions.[16] The differential is not found to the same degree in better organized countries.

Whether unions are able to raise wages in a macroeconomic sense is a difficult question to answer. Would the level of wages in most countries be lower than they are now in the absence of unions? Economists have been arguing about this for many years without reaching a consensus. Standard economic theory has it that unions can only raise wages above free market levels through the exercise of monopoly power, which would not be a factor with a high degree of organization. A counterargument is that unions can raise productivity by improving the industrial relations climate, among other things, thus enlarging the space for market-determined wages.

Another facet of the problem prevails where industrywide or even national collective bargaining exists. Unions have often been prepared to limit their wage demands to increases in the cost of living in order to prevent inflation, particularly when an allied political party is in office. A good example is the 1983 Australian Accord.[17] This practice confronts unions with a serious problem that is a direct consequence of their economic power. If they do not join government and employers in a stabilization pact, they may be held responsible for inflation. If the leadership is convinced that stablization is in the long-term interest of the unions, they risk loss of membership confidence. Left-wing opponents may castigate responsible leaders for lack of militancy.

The universal enactment of minimum wage laws reduces the impetus for low-paid workers to organize in order to secure a living wage. The union role in winning such legislation is often overlooked.

The growth of international trade and competition may also work against union influence. Unions tend to favor protectionist tariff policies in order to preserve domestic wages and jobs. However, unions in export industries tend to support free trade, so there is no clear perception of what the movement as a whole stands for on this issue.

Union leaders are convinced that they contribute to rising wage levels, and this is an important talking point in membership drives. What is more important is what potential members think. The opinion polls cited in Chapter 7 shed some light on this question. In Canada, few of those polled believed that securing higher wages was an important union function. In Great Britain, only 20 percent thought that gaining higher wages was an advantage of union membership. Only 31 percent of Australian employees polled agreed that unions were good at providing higher wages, and the figure was 25 percent in New Zealand. All the available polls suggest that unions have lost the reputation they once enjoyed as the major vehicles for wage improvement. Bouts of wage-restraint episodes that have occurred in most countries have made employees more sophisticated about the macroeconomics of wages.

An important caveat should be entered for the developing countries, many of which are still far from the welfare state level. Wages are typically low, not far above subsistence, and employment in a unionized establishment may mean a substantial wage differential over not only nonunion enterprise but also against compensation in the informal sector. All these countries have minimum wage laws, but enforcement is another matter. It is fairly common for wages to be determined by government rather than by the market. When wages are let loose and unions given freedom to operate, it is not uncommon for wage levels to take a sharp upward turn. The prospect of higher wages remains a powerful incentive for union organization in developing countries.

Hours of Work

All industrialized countries have enacted legislation limiting hours of work. About half specify a norm of 40 hours a week or less. Some countries still have a standard 48-hour week, but collective agreements generally bring the level down to 40 hours. The norm in Britain, although not by legislation, is 39 hours. Overtime work is paid at penalty rates.

A reduction of working hours has been a major union objective in Germany. In 1984, the Metal Workers' Union mounted the biggest strike in postwar Germany and won a 38.5-hour settlement. A threatened strike in 1989 led to an agreement that the 35-hour week would be introduced in the industry in 1993. With this, the union declared that working time had ceased to be an active issue.

The British engineering unions gained a reduction to 39 hours in 1979 and began a campaign a decade later for 35 hours. An employer offer of a three-stage reduction of 30 minutes a year was rejected, and individual companies were struck. In the end, some firms settled for a gradual two-year reduction in exchange for changes in work practices. In Japan, a country in which working hours are the highest of any major industrial nation, the Ministry of Labor took the initiative in bringing down working hours, which fell to an average 44-hour week in 1991.

The objective of reduced working hours is likely to remain on union agendas, because it seems to rate fairly high in worker priorities. Whether it is sufficient to make unions attractive is problematical. A problem is that once established in a major sector of the economy, the hour standard tends to spread without a great deal of union action. Sooner or later, the new standard becomes embodied in legislation, becoming a dead issue for a long period. The 40-hour week remained the norm for almost half a century without a great deal of agitation for revision.

As for the developing countries, a 48-hour week would be regarded as optimal by working people. Unions could gain a good deal of support by fighting for the issue. Some countries have legislated shorter hours, but enforcement is lax.

Safety and Health

Legislation governing occupational safety and health is universal in the industrial nations. Injuries on the job continue, and while fatalities have fallen, injuries have not. The crucial problem is enforcement, not legislation. If insufficient funds are allocated to the factory inspectorate, legislation is not of great value. There are no internationally comparative data on industrial accidents or the number of labor inspectors, which makes it difficult to assess the quality of safety administration. In the United States, trade unions have been embroiled in controversy with the federal Office of Safety and Health Administration over the effectiveness of the government's regulatory activity, and there has been recent controversy in other countries as well, including Canada.

This is an area in which unions can continue to play an important role. It is particularly the case in new industries that involve the use of potentially dangerous machinery and material. The ability of an employee to raise a grievance when confronted with an operation that he or she considers risky or unhealthy remains an important service that unions can render.

Health Insurance

Most industrialized countries have some form of state-supported health insurance. Health care programs were pioneered by unions and were important in attracting members. This was particularly true in the United States, where collective bargaining led to employer-financed programs. However, when government action generalizes health coverage, the original incentive to unionize disappears.

Unemployment Compensation

The first funds established to assist unemployed workers were union based. Like health insurance, these funds were gradually subsidized, then taken over by the state. There are still some union funds, but the money comes from the government, and it is not necessary to be a union member to receive benefits.

Pensions

Union pension funds were introduced later, but they too were supplanted by state systems. Every industrial nation now pays pensions on a universal basis, although the amounts vary greatly. In most countries, the benefit structure provides retired employees with an adequate standard of living; in others it must be supplemented by private schemes or individual savings. The United States and Japan are in the latter group. Bargained pensions have been a significant drawing card for American unions, but there have been problems with the adequacy of individual company funding, which reduces their attractiveness. Government insurance instituted to guarantee the eventual payment of benefits has proved expensive and has provided less than full assurance that contracted benefits will be paid.

The expansion of government welfare schemes has reduced the earlier drawing power of unions. Opinion polls suggest that employees do not rank union provision of welfare benefits high as reasons for joining, except in the United States, where a national health scheme was not yet in place in late 1993. In Canada, only 8 percent of poll respondents rated better pensions as an important union function; in Norway, they were near the bottom of the list; in Australia and New Zealand, they did not play an important role. However, improving health and safety conditions on the job emerged as a fairly important consideration in countries for which there are data—Britain, the United States, Norway, Australia, and New Zealand—suggesting that inadequate administration of relevant legislation has left the unions with an important function.

Welfare programs in the developing countries are still in their infancy. The following is a fair statement of one of the most important constituents of the welfare net: "Generally, the state of occupational safety and health in developing countries is much poorer than in industrialized countries. In some developing countries, conditions have become worse in certain respects. Competition for scarce resources within the context of economic slow-down has limited the application of corrective and preventive measures, such as ergonomics, for improving occupational safety and health."[18] Most of these countries have good protective legislation on their books but lack the resources to enforce it.

Unemployment compensation is rarely to be found. Given the nature of the employment problem in these countries, such schemes are not feasible. A common alternative is legally mandated severance pay so that a discharged employee has something to fall back on.

National pension plans are just beginning to be introduced. Malaysia actually has a social security system that dates to 1952, while Taiwan adopted one in 1984. Korea has yet to enact a program with wide coverage, and Thailand has still not even considered one. Some form of national health service is not uncommon, but where it exists, it is usually underfunded.

The trade unions in the developing world are normally not sufficiently wealthy to institute benefit programs. Wages are too low to finance contributory schemes. Once the unions have acquired some political power, however, they may be in a position to induce government action. This is the case in Argentina, Mexico, and India, as well as in Chile before and after Pinochet.

Grievances

Providing an avenue for airing grievances remains one of the most important trade union functions, yet even this has been impaired. Several factors are at work: the rise of workshop-level power, the growing sophistication of personnel managers, and the provision of alternative legal mechanisms.

In the past, it was generally the local union that processed grievances for its members. Backed by national union financial and technical assistance, alleged violations of collective agreements were policed by the locals. This is still the case in many countries, but solving many of the day-to-day problems that arise in factories and offices has devolved to a greater extent on factory committees that are not necessarily part of the union structure.

A few examples may clarify this trend. German works councils are an integral part of codetermination, and as such their constitution and authority are prescribed by law. Any employee in the enterprise may run for office and vote in council elections, regardless of union status. The councils may not call strikes or deal with wage and other issues covered by collective agreements, but they enjoy many other prerogatives. They must be consulted on working hours, vacation arrangements, safety and health regulations, social services, and principles of remuneration such as job evaluation and piecework rates. Their consent is necessary for hiring, promotions, and transfers. They must be consulted in advance for planned construction and for changes in working processes.

Japanese union structure makes it unnecessary to have separate workshop committees, because virtually all union authority is vested in the local enterprise union. These bodies bargain and consult on many issues, but they are less than equal partners in the bargaining process. They are entrusted with handling grievances, but despite elaborate grievance procedures contained in many collective agreements, few formal grievances are raised.

British industrial relations have been plagued with the consequences of multiple unionism and weak local union structure. Shop stewards, usually independent of unions, are elected by employees. They form committees that deal informally with employers on a wide range of issues and normally handle grievances. Their power to enforce their demands by calling strikes has been curbed by recent legislation, but unofficial work stoppages have not entirely disappeared. In Italy and Spain, quasi-independent factory councils provide a mechanism for settling grievances, and Canada has recently moved toward joint labor-management committees to minimize layoffs. Trade unions remain dominant at the workshop level in the United States, Australia, and New Zealand, although informal shop committees have developed recently in Australia with as-yet ill-defined functions.

The dilution of the union grievance function has been the result not only of the emergence of independent or quasi-union representation but also of employer policies and statutory regulation. Employers have adopted practices designed to convince employees that legitimate complaints will be taken care of on an individual basis. The change in terminology from *personnel* to *human resources* departments is symbolic of a more sophisticated management approach. There is increased recognition that employee morale is an important productivity factor and that it is counterproductive merely to suppress discontent. Particularly where skills are involved, the cost of recruitment and training is regarded as an investment that should be protected. Seniority in promotion and layoffs may be adopted without any union intercession.[19]

Illustrative of statutory regulation is legislation enacted by the Canadian federal government and several provinces protecting individuals against unjust dismissal, including the right of appeal to an impartial tribunal. Canadian unions have opposed the extension of such rights to nonunion firms because of their justified concern that unionization would be discouraged.

As stated at the outset of this section, grievance representation remains an important union function. But it is far from the situation that prevailed in earlier years. When U.S. unions sought to organize the mass production industries in the 1930s, their principal appeal was an intense feeling on the part of workers that they were being treated unfairly. The establishment of grievance machinery, not higher wages, was among the first union demands when collective bargaining began. Things have moved a long way since.

Trade Union Political Activity

A traditional union appeal was the possibility of achieving greater social equality by throwing the weight of union power behind socialist or labor parties. Ideology as well as economic benefit made unionization attractive.

The demise of communism and decline of socialism have reduced the ideological pull. When the German unions revived after World War II, they resolved to remain politically neutral rather than resume their prewar socialist ties, and they have done so. The century-old alliance between the unions and the Labour party in Britain is threatened by repeated Conservative electoral victories. There has been some agitation within Rengo, the new Japanese labor federation, to support individuals rather than left-wing parties. The largest of the Italian labor federations, long under communist control, has dissolved its political ties. Spain's principal union federation has all but severed its links to the governing Socialist Workers party.

Close relationships persist between the Australian Labor party and the Council of Trade Unions, and while there has been disarray within both the unions and the Labor party in New Zealand, connections have been maintained. The Canadian Labor Congress has kept its close links with the socialist New Democratic party, despite the latter's lack of success on the national political scene.

Although there are no formal ties between the AFL-CIO and the Democratic party, the unions have supported the Democratic candidate for president in every election but one since 1948, although a substantial number of union members vote Republican. There is nothing ideological about joining a union in the United States.

Most blue-collar workers continue to support parties on the left, but they do so as individuals rather than as union members. The old concept of a unified labor movement, with political and trade union wings, has been crumbling. Moreover, the relative growth of white-collar employment has greatly complicated the situation.

In only a handful of developing countries have unions been in a position to provide serious support to political parties. Latin America offers several examples – Argentina, Chile, and Mexico in the sample – but this is not the case in Africa or Asia, apart from India. The usual pattern is for political parties to establish and control nascent union movements for their own purposes. It will be some time before unions in the newly industrializing countries of Asia can play a role similar to that in the industrial nations.

The Scandinavian Exception

Reference has been made to the unique experience of the Scandinavian countries with respect to trade union density. Sweden and Norway were among the few industrial countries that did not suffer a density decline during the 1980s, although there was a moderate decline in Denmark. The three countries had the highest absolute density rates in 1988, and although caution must be exercised in making international comparisons, the differences are so great that the high rates are undoubtedly significant.

Moreover, it is the Scandinavian countries that have traveled furthest along the welfare state road, as Table 8.1 indicates. This appears to contradict the thesis that the transfer of welfare benefits and services from unions to government is a crucial factor in explaining density decline. What explains this apparent anomoly?

Several recent studies of employee attitudes toward unions in Sweden throw some light on the matter. First, there is the basic question of why employees are willing to join unions when they are surrounded by a state-supported safety net. Union members in Sweden were asked in 1985 what motivated them to unionize, with the following results:[20]

	LO	TCO	SACO
I joined because most other people are union members	13%	13%	11%
I felt I was compelled to go along	11	12	8
I personally benefited by joining	51	46	41
I believe in solidarity with the trade union world	23	28	37
Other	2	2	4

Recall that LO unions cater primarily to blue-collar workers, TCO to white-collar employees, and SACO to professionals with higher education. It is interesting that half the LO members joined because of expected personal benefits and less than half of those in TCO and SACO. Rather surprising, the ideological factor of union solidarity was strongest for SACO and weakest for LO. More education apparently does not mean greater individualism, at least in Sweden.

As a follow-up, the respondents were asked whether they had observed anyone being subjected to unpleasantness or insult for not joining a union:

	LO	TCO	SACO
Have noticed it	26%	26%	24%
Have not noticed it	71	73	76
Doubtful	3	1	0

Those who had observed some pressure were then asked what form it had taken:

	LO	TCO	SACO
Insults or other forms of oral pressure	60%	61%	69
Ostracism	12	9	12
Actions by members	14	11	6
Actions by union officials	10	13	10
Other	3	2	0
Do not know	2	3	3

There is some difference in the behavior of the more educated union members but not as much as might have been expected. Personal benefit remained a potent factor, but compulsion and ideology also played a role. But compulsion certainly did not have the same force as in countries with less powerful unions. In a country such as Sweden, which is almost completely organized, joining a union is almost like participating in political elections or exercising other obligations of citizenship. There is nothing controversial about it. Attaining an 85-percent density rate is the best protection that unions can have against decline. The problem is getting there.

Recall that almost half the respondents cited personal benefit as their reason for joining a union. The nature of the benefits emerged from another poll:[21]

	Most important issues	Unions should be concerned with them	High union achievment in this area
Increased fellowship on the job	48%	60%	28%
Increased job security	48	78	41
Lower taxes	41	54	7
Improved work environment	33	69	45
Higher wages	33	78	40
Greater wage influence on social policy	29	49	14
Increased codetermination	21	62	41

(These are tallies of multiple responses)

A 1991 poll conducted among members of the Swedish Metal Workers' Union, the second largest in the country, revealed a somewhat different list of preferences:[22]

	Union should work for	Union has done best here
Better working environment	50 %	31%
Higher wages	34	14
More job security	29	24
Support and help in grievances	19	13
Support in strikes and lockouts	15	13
Better and more interesting jobs	13	5
Influencing politicians	12	4
Shorter working hours	11	6

(Respondents were asked to list their two highest preferences)

Although wages ranked higher as important issues than in the general poll cited earlier, working environment was again at the top (if camaraderie is considered part of the working environment). Job security, which was omitted from the list of choices in the general poll, ranked not far below wages among the metal workers. The union is perceived of as having done least well on environmental issues.

A poll conducted in 1988 by the Swedish Central Statistical Bureau covering union members revealed that job security and wages were the most important issues for unions to deal with, followed closely by income loss during illness and unemployment and by the working environment. The ranking of employment benefits, apart from those contained in collective agreements, were subsidized lunches, the possibility of engaging in personal education at least once a year, free medical care, free coffee, access to exercise facilities, and the availability of goods and services at reduced prices. Among the general conclusions drawn from this survey were that Swedish employees wanted to be union members, that they wanted unions to have increased influence at the workplace, and that LO members did not favor any weakening of cooperation with the Social Democratic party, although they opposed stronger ties.[23]

The success of Swedish unionism depended on the initial ability of blue-collar workers to achieve a near-saturation level of density. This was done in collaboration with a political party that held power for a long period of time, with few interruptions. During their joint tenure, a comprehensive social welfare program was installed. To finance the program, high taxes were levied, among the highest in the world. White-collar employees and professionals began to realize that it was in their interest to unionize, if only as protection against having to shoulder more than a proportionate share of the tax burden. Moreover, the blue-collar workers were in a position to exact wage increases with a minimum of employer resistance, sometimes at their expense.

These groups were organized separately from the older unions. They were not prepared to ally with the Social Democratic party and remained politically neutral. Initially taking a defensive stance, the new federations eventually became more aggressive in defending the interests of their members. They participated, as did the LO, in major macroeconomic policy debates involving the government, including the level and allocation of taxes among different income groups, government subsidy of consumer goods, and income policies.

The agenda of Swedish unions differ considerably from those of unions in other countries. They are quasigovernment bodies endowed with a good deal of authority. One of the public opinion polls cited had this to say about them: "The function of the trade unions was to advance the wages of their members. The wage struggle was and is their most important task. But taxes and deductions are now and have long been at such a level that a small portion of membership standards can be influenced through wage setting. . . . A union can no longer fill its original tasks and there are difficulties in shaping a new role . . . and those that do not do so are met with rising distrust. They lose their legitimacy."[24]

It is clear from the opinion polls cited that Swedish union members expect of their organizations a wider range of services than are generally found in other countries, including improvement in the working environment, tax relief, and greater access to corporate decision making. Even health and safety on the job take on different aspects; by law rather than contract, in all but the smallest firms employees elect safety shop stewards who are empowered to shut down any process or rule out any materials that they consider potentially dangerous *before* government inspectors are called in to investigate.

For these reasons, among others, a density decline of any magnitude is not anticipated. The mechanism by which gaps in union membership are filled is almost automatic. The growing number of service-sector employees are accommodated in unions specializing in their requirements — women as well as men, those at different educational levels, diplomats and secretaries, physicians and police officials, and even regular military officers.

Does the Swedish model also characterize the other Scandinavian countries? There are many similarities among them that can lead to a positive answer. All have organized a large proportion of service personnel and women. There tend to be separate labor federations. Norway has 218,000 members in unions of lawyers, engineers, economists, dentists, and midwives, among others, while in Denmark there are 325,000 in the independent Civil Service and Salaried Employees Federation.

In these countries the major union concerns have shifted from the traditional wages and hours. Some form of codetermination exists in all three countries, and the working environment and job security are major concerns. The unions have assumed some responsibility for macroeconomic policy and have had to come to grips with the problems faced in remaining competitive in foreign markets.

There are differences among the Scandinavian unions stemming from their history and traditions as well as the structure of their economies, and it has been argued that the term *Scandinavian model* is misleading.[25] Nevertheless, by comparison with other countries, the Scandinavian unions bear a striking resemblance to one another. There is a distinctive Scandinavian model that has pioneered the road to a high density of organization.

THE FUTURE OF TRADE UNIONISM

To recapitulate: The various factors that have been cited in the literature to explain differences in union density decline among industrial nations—economic growth rates; industrial restructuring; differences in earning trends, female employment, government policies, and employer attitudes—do not prove significant when international comparisons are made. Unemployment and union quality are significant but explain only a minor portion of the differences. What is more, a multivariate analysis in which all the variables were regressed against density did not yield significant results. For the developing countries, none of the variables was significant.

To emphasize what has been said earlier, this does not mean that particular factors are not determining in individual countries. Various studies that have been cited show that they are. The problem is that the same variable—industrial restructuring, for example—may have quite different effects on union density among countries.

Of more general import is that the traditional union agendas of higher wages, shorter hours, grievance adjustment, pensions, and medical insurance have been preempted by government and are provided to all citizens, regardless of union status.

Many unions have begun to realize what has happened and to attempt to expand their offerings to new fields. The AFL-CIO, for example, initiated the Union Privilege Benefit Program in which it sought to put a group of goods and services normally purchased in the marketplace under the union umbrella. Included were credit cards; legal services; life, health, and automobile insurance; planning and investing for retirement; and travel assistance.

The difficulty with this program is that it operates in an extremely competitive area. Credit cards are available at the nearest bank. Legal services are widely advertised on television, among other media. Insurance and financial advice has been on the market for many years, and the same is true of travel services. Some union members may subscribe to the union offers, but the services are not likely to attract new members; the benefits are not sufficiently great.

In fact, a number of similar services have been offered by European unions, some for many years. Among them are building societies to assist in home financing; union banks, travel agencies, and vacation resorts; book clubs; and educational facilities. Consumer cooperatives enjoyed strong union support when they were initiated, but they tended to fade with the rise of supermarkets operating on thin profit margins. Living a "union life," surrounded by union institutions, was once possible. It no longer is.

What has emerged from evaluating the problems faced by the labor movements of the industrial nations is that forces are at work that will require fundamental changes in the way unions are structured and operated if the downward trends in density are to be reversed. The causes lie in great shifts in the composition of the labor force that have taken place during the last few decades and the emergence of the welfare state.

The Labor Force

It is hardly necessary to stress the labor force as a factor. The average level of educational attainment has risen in every country. Unemployment has led to a greater emphasis on skill training to meet the staffing needs of the new high-technology industries. Many countries have relied on immigration from the developing countries to supply unskilled labor, because domestic employees are largely skilled. The manufacturing industries that survive do so on the basis of advancing technology, leading to increased production with reduced labor participation. What is left of unskilled labor is to be found in service industries that are difficult to mechanize.

This means that union organizers face a much more sophisticated clientele than at any time in the past. The contemporary labor force is almost completely literate and has easy access to information. The so-called money illusion used to be cited as an anti-inflationary factor but no more; almost everyone knows the difference between money and real wages. Moreover, with rising productivity has come rising afflu-

ence. Not everyone is wealthy by any means, but few employed people
are near poverty levels.

More education and higher incomes have led to rising expectations,
not necessarily limited to more money. The opinion polls have suggested
that to attract contemporary employees, blue-collar and white-collar
alike, unions will have to offer a different menu of services than that
which proved successful at an earlier stage of development. They need
new products, as every successful entrepreneur has learned.

Employment Security

The high unemployment that prevailed in the OECD countries during the 1980s exacerbated the fear of being without a job. All sectors
of the labor force were affected, even management. From 1974 to 1979,
the average rate of unemployment for member nations of the OECD
was 4.9 percent, rising to 7.3 percent from 1980 to 1989. For the latter
period, Britain averaged 10 percent, Spain 17.5 percent, Canada 9.3
percent, France 9 percent, and Italy 10.9 percent. Concern about wage
levels pales against the prospect of total cessation of income.

Unions have begun to realize this. Collective bargaining has already
taken some steps in the direction of greater job security. A recent
agreement between the Canadian Auto Workers and the major auto
manufacturers requires the companies to give one year's notice of
plant closures and early retirement with full pension for workers with
at least 10 years of service. There are also two to three years of income
protection, depending on length of service, or severance pay from
$25,000 to $65,000 (Canadian dollars).

Most countries have legislated advance notification and severance
pay, and there was a short-lived attempt in France to prohibit layoffs
without government permission. The only country in which employees
of large enterprises have tenure is Japan. This was instituted unilater-
ally by the employers after a tumultuous decade of industrial strife
during the 1950s, and it served its purpose. Japanese workers have ac-
quiesced in employer domination ever since in return for the assurance
that they will not be laid off until retirement. This promise is the linch-
pin of the Japanese industrial relations system and protects employers
against militant unionism.

Few considerations would attract workers to unions as much as
union aid in a guarantee of stable employment. The question is how
this can be reconciled with a dynamic economy. Firms come and go, expand and contract. In fact, substantial groups of employees already
enjoy some measure of long-term job tenure: employees of national and
local governments and teachers at all levels, in the private as well as
the public sector. There have also been some commitments by private

enterprises, but many of these have fallen by the wayside as a consequence of the recession that set in during the late 1980s.

Given a growing reaction against unemployment and the political costs of ignoring it, it is not unlikely that ways will be found to extend job protection to more segments of the labor force. By putting this issue at the top of their agendas and attempting to formulate feasible bargaining demands, unions might retrieve some of the momentum they enjoyed in earlier years.

Participation in Enterprise Decision Making

The quest for democracy at the workplace is more than a century old and has taken many forms. The most recent scheme, codetermination, originated in postwar Germany and spread to the Scandinavian countries, among others. It has worked well for 40 years and proved to be compatible with economic efficiency.

The basic idea is that all employees should participate in business decisions that affect their jobs and income. This would include changes in technology, new products, mergers and acquisitions, plant closures and relocation, reductions in force, and even managerial compensation. Moreover, the participation would not be merely advisory but would be fortified by some degree of mandatory authority.

To prevent employer domination, the instruments of employee participation would have to go beyond the level of the individual firm, and national unions are ideally suited for this function. They have a broader view of the economy and of the situation of any single firm within an industry than an in-house works council can have. An additional argument for some form of codetermination is that it is a powerful lever for the protection of jobs. Corporate personnel decisions are often made without adequate consideration of alternatives and too frequently by new managers who are brought in to strengthen weak enterprises. The experience of Germany and the Scandinavian countries has shown that boards of directors that include employee representatives can produce a rational layoff policy that takes into consideration the value of human as well as physical capital.

Unions in Great Britain and the United States, among others, have traditionally opposed this form of employee participation in principle. Their concern is that employees may become too attached to individual firms, thus impairing their loyalty to the union. Let managers manage, and let the union extract as much as possible for its members – that is the attitude they have taken. This seems very shortsighted in view of increasing employee resentment at being treated as expendable by management. Unions that do not press for participatory schemes are denying themselves a potent organizing weapon.

Independent Organization

The key to achieving higher membership density is the organization of service-sector employees who are supplanting those engaged in manufacturing. Where this has been successful, as in Scandinavia and other countries, it has been done on the basis of specialized unions that cater to the particular interests of the various occupational groups. The earliest unions in the West were all based on craft, and many have survived.

The idea that large industrial unions promote worker solidarity and raise their bargaining power may have been valid when the mass production industries were forming into large enterprise units, but it may be counterproductive today. The interests of different occupational groups may diverge and even come into sharp conflict on some issues. Employees in industries that are heavy exporters are likely to have a completely different view of free trade than those that face competition from imports. Even people working in the same establishment may find themselves on the opposite side of the bargaining table—for example, highly skilled physicians and nurses versus semiskilled hospital personnel.

This means that the efforts of the traditional unions to compensate for their membership losses by entering into unrelated areas of work are not likely to pay off. Organization of the specialized service groups will probably come from within when practitioners perceive a need. Academic and trade associations may be transformed into collective bargaining organizations, the origin of many of the newer unions. The largest union of teachers in the United States, the National Education Association, which remains independent of the AFL-CIO, is a good example. Professionals are often reluctant to enter the same organizations as blue-collar workers, but they will join their own associations when their interests are threatened.

The Work Environment

A high priority activity that employees expect of their unions is obtaining improved working conditions. This is apart from health and safety issues, the pursuit of which is taken for granted.

Improvement can mean many things, depending upon the nature of the industry and occupation involved. In its most ambitious sense, it can place upon employers the obligation to adapt working conditions to human physical and mental capabilities and arrange work so that employees can influence the work situation. An example from the automobile industry entails abolition of straight assemblyline work in favor of breaking the productive process down into larger units that involve a greater range of tasks performed by individuals and more worker control over the timing of each operation.

Improvement can also mean better atmospheric, acoustical, and light conditions. Clean facilities for meals and good food where meals are served should be provided by employers without union intervention, but they often are not. A sore point that unions can use to their advantage is the contrast that often exists between luxurious dining rooms that are open only to management and shoddy staff canteens. In general, today's more educated labor force can be expected to demand greater equality in all the facilities available at the place of work, including parking, recreation, and access to the perquisites that are provided to management. They are not satisfied with treatment as second-class citizens, either in their daily life or at work.

Women Employees

The postwar years have been marked by an almost revolutionary increase in the level of female labor force participation. The reasons are not entirely clear, but the consequences are evident. Women have special employment problems to which neither employers nor unions have reacted adequately.

One of these is the necessity of part-time work for women who have children. Instead of facilitating the adjustment of working hours to fit women's needs, many unions have opposed part-time work. For example, in Germany, the Public Service Workers' Union, which had long sought to discourage part-time employment, only recently negotiated an agreement with public authorities regularizing the arrangement. A 1987 survey taken in the United States revealed that about three-quarters of the women working part time were doing so voluntarily, not because they were unable to find full-time work. Unions in some countries have advocated part-time work as a palliative for unemployment, but this is not at all the same thing and may be unwise.

The U.S. Labor Department reported recently that more than 1 million young mothers did not seek or hold jobs because of the lack of affordable quality child care.[26] The moral of this story for unions is obvious: The establishment of union-sponsored day-care centers would be a powerful attraction for younger people and cement their loyalty to the union. These need not be overly costly and are good investments.

The density rate for women is lower than for men in every country for which there are data, except Denmark and Sweden, where they are the same. There is a prevalent notion that women are somehow less apt to join unions than men, but this is not true. Under similar circumstances, they are equally interested in joining unions. Their degree of organization is related to their occupations and their heavy representation in services that are not unionized for different reasons. The decline of union density owes a great deal to the failure of unions to make special efforts to involve women.

Trade Union Government

The opinion polls reveal some dissatisfaction, on the part of members and nonmembers alike, with the way unions are governed. More than one-half of those who responded to an Australian poll said that unions were doing a poor job in giving members a say in how a union is run, and more than 40 percent felt that unions had fallen down in telling members what the unions were doing. There were similar results in New Zealand, Great Britain, and the United States.

This is again a reflection of the reaction of a more highly educated labor force. In the past, branding union officials as dictatorial or corrupt was shrugged off by members as employer propaganda designed to weaken the union. Moreover, particularly in a class-conscious society, unions were conceived of as quasimilitary bodies in which strong leadership and unquestioning member loyalty were essential to success. This is no longer true; the proliferation of information sources puts a much heavier burden on union leaders to justify their policies and explain why unions are run as they are.

Political Affiliations

Close formal ties between trade unions and political parties are not as popular as they once were. The German unions solved the problem by opting for political neutrality when they were reorganized after World War II. The French and Italian unions have suffered because of their ideological divisions. The issue is under debate in Britain. The Swedish experience drives the point home: Organization of the service sector mandates political neutrality if it is to take place.

Not all blue-collar workers vote automatically for labor parties, nor do white-collar people vote overwhelmingly conservative. But a substantial majority of the latter do support conservative parties, and it would be folly to expect them to join organizations committed to labor. Moreover, objections to their neutrality miss an important point: Should white-collar employees organize under the banners of political independence, they can play an important role in guaranteeing a level playing field in collective bargaining. If service employees in Britain and the United States were as well organized as in Sweden, it is hardly likely that the Thatcher and Reagan-Bush administrations could have been as pro-employer as they were. The blue-collar unions have a large stake in white-collar unionization, regardless of its political hue.

SUMMARY

There is no guarantee that adoption by trade unions of any one or combination of the agenda items that now appear to be of particular interest to members or prospective members will arrest the decline of union density. Decline could continue despite commitment to these or other objectives. An outstanding example is what has happened in Germany despite a strong union commitment to participatory democracy in industry. Moreover, particular economic or political circumstances in individual countries may render new approaches impractical.

What can be said, however, is that continued reliance on traditional appeals are not likely to serve the cause of trade unionism well. Unions are well advised to consider more carefully the special interests of those whom they would like to represent, particularly the various groups of skilled workers, service employees, and women. This may entail a revision of prevailing attitudes and current operational modes, but it is probably the best way to turn the trend of union density upward once more.

Little of the foregoing applies to unions in the developing countries. They have a long way to go before the traditional concentration on wages and hours loses its appeal. Where there is economic growth and a modicum of political democracy, they are thriving. Their problem is to establish themselves as independent representatives of employee welfare, to shake off government and employer domination, and to gain social legitimacy.

Asian unions, particularly those in such newly industrialized countries as Korea and Taiwan, are still in the upward swing of the membership density curve that characterized Western unionism during the century between 1850 and 1950. It may be another half century before they reach the apogee of that curve and have to modify the character of their appeals.

NOTES

1. For a comprehensive review of the literature, see Gary N. Chaison and Joseph B. Rose, "The Macrodeterminants of Union Growth and Decline," in George Strauss, et al., eds., *The State of the Unions* (Madison, Wis.: Industrial Relations Research Association, 1990), p. 3.

2. Henry S. Farber, "The Decline of Unionization in the United States," *Journal of Labor Economics* 8 (1990): S 75.

3. Richard B. Freeman, "Contraction and Expansion," *Journal of Economic Perspectives,* Spring 1988, p. 221.

4. Jeremy Waddington, "Trade Union Membership in Britain, 1980–1987," *British Journal of Industrial Relations,* June 1992, p. 313.

5. Richard B. Freeman and Jeffrey Pelletier, "The Impact of Industrial

Relations Legislation on British Union Density," *British Journal of Industrial Relations*, July 1990, p. 156.

6. Brian Towers, "Running the Gauntlet: British Trade Unions under Thatcher," *Industrial and Labor Relations Review*, January 1989, p. 163.

7. Richard Disney, "Explanation of the Decline in Trade Union Density in Britain," *British Journal of Industrial Relations*, July 1990, p. 165.

8. Jeff Bridgeford, "French Trade Unions: Crisis in the 1980s," *Industrial Relations Journal*, Spring 1990, p. 126.

9. David Peetz, "Declining Union Density," *Journal of Industrial Relations*, June 1990, p. 197.

10. Jonathan Reshef, "Union Decline: A View from Canada," *Journal of Labor Research*, Winter 1990, p. 25.

11. Bert Klandermans, "Psychology and Trade Union Participation," *Journal of Occupational Psychology*, 1986, p. 189.

12. Hoyt N. Wheeler and John A. McClendon, "The Individual Decision to Unionize," in Strauss et al., eds., *State of the Unions*, p. 77.

13. Henry Pelling, *A History of British Trade Unionism* (New York: Penguin Books, 1949), p. 47.

14. Philip Taft, *The AF of L in the Time of Gompers* (New York: Harper & Bros., 1957), pp. 142–143.

15. Quoted in Selig Perlman, *A Theory of the Labor Movement* (New York: Augustus M. Kelley, 1949), p. 80.

16. Some unions have agreed to a two-tiered wage system in which current employees are paid on the existing scale and new employees on a lower one. Nothing could be designed to destroy a union as effectively as this practice.

17. See Shaun Carney, *Australia in Accord* (Melbourne: Sun Books, 1988).

18. International Labour Office, *World Labor Report* (Geneva: ILO, 1985), p. 143.

19. See Thomas Kochan, Robert McKersie, and John Chalykoff, "The Effects of Corporate Strategy and Workplace Innovations on Union Representation," *Industrial and Labor Relations Review*, July 1986, p. 487.

20. Anders Leion, *Sjalsfrandskap och Medlemskap* (Stockholm: SIFO Opinion, 1987), pp. 136–137.

21. Leion, *Sjalsfrandskap och Medlemskap*, p. 167.

22. *Medlems Undersokning i Metall* (Stockholm: SIFO, December 1991), p. 14.

23. *Röster om Facket och Jobbet* (Stockholm: LO, 1988), pp. 65–73.

24. Leion, *Sjalsfrandskap och Medlemskap*, p. 103.

25. See, for example, Arvid Fennefoss and Torgeir Stokke, "Norske Lonnstakers Organisering," *Sokelyst po Arbeidsmarkedet*, No. 2, 1991, pp. 132–134.

26. *Monthly Labor Review*, October 1991, p. 3.

References

Armstrong, E. G. A. "Employer Associations in Great Britain." In *Employers Associations and Industrial Relations*, eds. John T. Windmuller and Allan Gladstone. Oxford, England: Clarendon Press, 1984.

Australian Bureau of Statistics. *Trade Union Membership in Australia*. Canberra: Australian Bureau of Statistics, 1990.

Avniceldin, Marilyn. *Malaysian Industrial Relations*. Singapore: McGraw-Hill, 1990.

Barrera, Manuel, Helia Henriquez, and Tereseta Selame. *Trade Unions and the State in Present Day Chile*. Geneva: United Nations Research Institute for Social Development, pp. 65–68.

Beaumont, P. B. *Changes in Industrial Relations*. London: Routledge, 1990.

Bengoccha, Sagardoy, and David Leon Blanco. *El Poder Sindical en Espana*, 1982, p. 71.

Bridgeford, Jeff. "French Trade Unions: Crisis in the 1980s." *Industrial Relations Journal*, Spring 1990, p. 126.

Bunn, Ronald F. "Employer Associations in the Federal Republic of Germany." In *Employers Associations and Industrial Relations*, eds. John T. Windmuller and Allan Gladstone. Oxford, England: Clarendon Press, 1984.

Calvi, Gabriele. *Indagina Sociala Italiana*. Milan: Franco Angeli, 1987.

Carney, Shaun. *Australia in Accord*. Melbourne: Sun Books, 1988.

Chaison, Gary N., and Joseph B. Rose. "The Macrodeterminants of Union Growth and Decline." In George Strauss et al., *The State of the Unions*. Madison, Wis.: Industrial Relations Research Association, 1990.

Chang, Clara, and Constance Sorrentino. "Union Membership Statistics in 12 Countries." *Monthly Labor Review*, December 1991, p. 46.

Commission of the European Communities. *Young Europeans in 1987*. Brussels, 1989.

Crouch, Colin. "United Kingdom: The Rejection of Compromise." In *European Industrial Relations*, eds. Guido Baglioni and Colin Crouch. London: Sage, 1990.

Disney, Richard. "Explanation of the Decline in Trade Union Density in Britain." *British Journal of Industrial Relations*, July 1990, p. 165.

Duffy, Norman F. "Employers Associations in Australia." In *Employers Associations and Industrial Relations*, eds. John T. Windmuller and Allan Gladstone. Oxford, England: Clarendon Press, 1984.

Edwards, P. K., and George Sayers Bain. "Why Are Trade Unions Becoming More Popular? Unions and Public Opinion in Britain." *British Journal of Industrial Relations*, November 1988.

Epstein, Edward C. *Labor Autonomy and the State in Latin America.* Boston: Unwin Hyman, 1989.

Estivill, Jordi, and Joseph P. M. de la Hoz. "Transition and Crisis: The Complexity of Spanish Industrial Relations." In *European Industrial Relations*, eds. Guido Baglioni and Colin Crouch. London: Sage, 1990.

Farber, Henry. "The Decline of Unionization in the United States." *Journal of Labor Economics* 8 (1990) S 75.

Fennefoss, Arvid. *Wage Earner Organization*, FAFO Report No. 081. Oslo: FAFO, 1988.

Fennefoss, Arvid, and Torgeir Stokke. "Norske Lonnstakers Organisering." *Sokelyst po Arbeidsmarkedet*, No. 2, 1991, pp. 132–134.

Freeman, Richard. "Contraction and Expansion." *Journal of Economic Perspectives*, Spring 1988.

Freeman, Richard, and James L. Medoff. *What Do Unions Do?* New York: Basic Books, 1985.

Freeman, Richard, and Jeffrey Pelletier. "The Impact of Industrial Relations Legislation on British Union Density." *British Journal of Industrial Relations*, July 1990, p. 142.

Gallup Organization. *1988 Gallup Survey of Public Opinion about Labor Issues.* Princeton, N.J.: Gallup.

Goldfield, Michael. *The Decline of Organized Labor in the United States.* Chicago: University of Chicago Press, 1987, p. 225.

Grant, W., and D. Marsh. *The CBI.* London: Holder and Stoughton, 1977.

Hyman, Richard. *Strikes.* London: Macmillan, 1989.

Inagami, Takeshi. "The Growth of the Service Economy." *Japan Labor Bulletin*, March 1985.

Index to International Public Opinion, various issues.

Industrial Relations Center. *The New Zealand System of Industrial Relations.* University of Wellington, 1989.

Industrial Relations Research Association. *The State of the Unions.* Madison, Wis.: Industrial Relations Research Association, 1991.

International Gallup Polls, various issues.

International Labour Office. *The Cost of Social Security.* Geneva: ILO, 1986.

——. *World Labor Report.* Geneva: ILO, 1985 and 1990.

Jacobi, Otto, and Walter Muller-Jentsch. "West Germany." In *European Industrial Relations*, eds. Guido Baglioni and Colin Crouch. London: Sage, 1990.

Japan Institute of Labor. *Japanese Working Life in Profile.* Tokyo: Japan Institute of Labor, 1992.

Karlsen, Jan Erik. *Hva Skjer i Fagbevegelsen.* Oslo: Tiden Norsk Forlag, 1977.

Klandermans, Bert. "Psychology and Trade Union Participation." *Journal of Occupational Psychology,* 1986, p. 189.

Kleingartner, Archie, and Hseuh-yu Peng. *Taiwan: A Study of Labor Relations in Transition.* Los Angeles: Institute of Industrial Relations, University of California, 1990.

Kochan, Thomas, Robert McKersie, and John Chalykoff. "The Effects of Corporate Strategy and Workplace Innovations on Union Representation." *Industrial and Labor Relations Review,* July 1986, p. 487.

Kumar, Pradeep. *Industrial Relations in Canada and the United States.* Kingston, Ontario, Canada: Queen's University, 1991.

Kumar, Pradeep, and Dennis Ryan (eds.). *Canadian Labor Movement in the 1980s.* Kingston, Ontario, Canada: Queen's University, 1988.

Lane, Christel. *Management and Labor in Europe.* Aldershot, England: Edward Elgar, 1980.

Leion, Anders. *Sjalsfrandskap och Medlemskap.* Stockholm: SIFO Opinion, 1987.

Lewin, Leif. *Governing Trade Unions in Sweden.* Cambridge, Mass.: Harvard University Press, 1980.

McElrath, Roger C. *Trade Unions and the Industrial Relations Climate in Spain.* Philadelphia: Wharton School, 1989.

Murray, Gregor. *Canadian Unions and Economic Restructuring.* Kingston, Ontario, Canada: Queen's University, 1991.

New Zealand System of Industrial Relations. Wellington: Industrial Relations Center, 1989, p. 108.

Noblecourt, Michael. *Les Syndicats en Question.* Paris: Les Éditions Ouvrières, 1990.

Norwegian Federation of Labor. *Temabok.* Oslo: Norwegian Federation of Labor, 1991.

Ogle, George E. *Korea: Dissent within the Economic Miracle.* London: Zed Books, 1990.

Organization for Economic Cooperation and Development. *Employment Outlook.* Paris: Organization for Economic Cooperation and Development, July 1991, p. 101.

——. *Main Economic Indicators – Historical Statistics.* Paris: Organization for Economic Cooperation and Development, 1982.

——. *Labour Force Statistics, 1969–1989.* Paris: Organization for Economic Cooperation and Development, 1991.

——. *Trends in Developing Economies.* Paris: Organization for Economic Cooperation and Development, 1990.

Peetz, David. "Declining Union Density." *Journal of Industrial Relations,* June 1990, p. 197.

Pelling, Henry. *A History of British Trade Unionism.* New York: Penguin Books, 1949.

Perlman, Selig. *A Theory of the Labor Movement.* New York: Augustus M. Kelley, 1949.

Pontusson, Jonas, and Savosh Kuruvilla. "Swedish Wage Earner Funds: An

Experiment in Economic Democracy." *Industrial and Labor Relations Review,* July 1992, p. 779.

Ramaswamy, E. A. *Power and Justice.* Delhi: Oxford University Press, 1984.

Ramaswamy, E. A., and Uma Ramaswamy. *Industry and Labor.* Delhi: Oxford University Press, 1981.

Ratnam, C. S. Venkata. *The Employer's Dilemma.* Bombay: Solar Foundation, 1989.

Rawson, D. W. *Unions and Unionism in Australia.* Sydney: Allen & Unwin, 1985.

Reshef, Jonathan. "Union Decline: A View from Canada." *Journal of Labor Research,* Winter 1990, p. 25.

Roiser, Martin, and Tim Little. "Public Opinion, Trade Unions and Industrial Relations." *Journal of Occupational Psychology* 59 (1986): 259.

Savery, Lawson K., and Geoffrey N. Soutar. *Trade Union Effectiveness.* Western Australian Labor Market Research Center, 1990.

Shirai, Tashio. *Contemporary Industrial Relations in Japan.* Madison: University of Wisconsin Press, 1983.

Smith, E. Owen. *Trade Unions in the Developed Economies.* New York: St. Martin's Press, 1981.

Stepino, Lee P., and Jack Fiorito. "Toward a Comprehensive Theory of Union Growth and Decline." *Industrial Relations,* Fall 1986, p. 259.

Taft, Philip. *The A F of L in the Time of Gompers.* New York: Harper & Bros., 1957.

Thompson, Mark. "Canadian Industrial Relations." In *International Comparative Industrial Relations,* eds. Gregg J. Bamber and Russel D. Lansbury. London: Allen & Unwin, 1987.

Tolliday, Steven, and Jonathan Zeitlin. *The Power to Manage.* London: Routledge, 1991.

Towers, Brian. "Running the Gauntlet: British Trade Unions under Thatcher." *Industrial and Labor Relations Review,* January 1989, p. 163.

Troy, Leo. "Is the U.S. Unique in the Decline of Private Sector Unionism?" *Journal of Labor Research,* Spring 1990, p. 115.

U.S. Department of Labor. *Foreign Labor Trends: Argentina, 1990.* Washington, D.C.: Government Printing Office, 1990.

——. *Foreign Labor Trends: Brazil, 1989.* Washington, D.C.: Government Printing Office, 1989.

——. *Foreign Labor Trends: France, 1989–1990.* Washington, D.C.: Government Printing Office, 1990.

——. *Foreign Labor Trends: Germany, 1990.* Washington, D.C.: Government Printing Office, 1990.

——. *Foreign Labor Trends: India, 1989–1990.* Washington, D.C.: Government Printing Office, 1990.

——. *Foreign Labor Trends: India, 1990–1991.* Washington, D.C.: Government Printing Office, 1991.

——. *Foreign Labor Trends: Italy, 1989–1990.* Washington, D.C.: Government Printing Office, 1990.

——. *Foreign Labor Trends: Kenya, 1987–1988.* Washington, D.C.: Government Printing Office, 1988.

——. *Foreign Labor Trends: Korea, 1990–1991.* Washington, D.C.: Government Printing Office, 1991.

——. *Foreign Labor Trends: Malaysia, 1988-1989.* Washington, D.C.: Government Printing Office, 1989.

——. *Foreign Labor Trends: Malaysia, 1990-1991.* Washington, D.C.: Government Printing Office, 1991.

——. *Foreign Labor Trends: Nigeria, 1987-1988.* Washington, D.C.: Government Printing Office, 1988.

——. *Foreign Labor Trends: Nigeria, 1990-1991.* Washington, D.C.: Government Printing Office, 1991.

——. *Foreign Labor Trends: Norway, 1989-1991.* Washington, D.C.: Government Printing Office, 1991.

——. *Foreign Labor Trends: Philippines, 1988-1989.* Washington, D.C.: Government Printing Office, 1989.

——. *Foreign Labor Trends: Philippines, 1990-1991.* Washington, D.C.: Government Printing Office, 1991.

——. *Foreign Labor Trends: Spain, 1989-1990.* Washington, D.C.: Government Printing Office, 1990.

——. *Foreign Labor Trends: Sweden, 1989-1990.* Washington, D.C.: Government Printing Office, 1990.

——. *Foreign Labor Trends: Taiwan, 1989.* Washington, D.C.: Government Printing Office, 1989.

——. *Foreign Labor Trends: Taiwan, 1990-1991.* Washington, D.C.: Government Printing Office, 1991.

——. *Foreign Labor Trends: Thailand, 1990-1991.* Washington, D.C.: Government Printing Office, 1991.

Visser, Jelle. *European Trade Unions in Figures.* Deventer, The Netherlands: Kluwers, 1989.

——. "Trends in Union Membership." Organization for Economic Cooperation and Development. *Employment Outlook,* July 1991.

Waddington, Jeremy. "Trade Union Membership in Britain, 1980-1987." *British Journal of Industrial Relations,* June 1992.

Wheeler, Hoyt N., and John A. McClendon, "The Individual Decision to Unionize." In George Strauss et al., *The State of the Unions.* Madison, Wis.: Industrial Relations Research Association, 1991.

World Bank. *World Development Report.* Washington, D.C.: World Bank, 1991.

——. *World Tables.* Washington, D.C.: World Bank, 1991.

Zieger, Robert H. *American Workers, American Unions, 1920-1985.* Baltimore: Johns Hopkins University Press, 1986.

Index

American Federation of Labor-
Congress of Industrial Organization (AFL-CIO), 29, 40; political
action, 76-77
Argentina: government-union relations, 41; public opinion about
unions, 116; union federations, 41;
union membership, 5
Attitudes toward union power:
Sweden, 128; United Kingdom,
127; United States, 128
Australia: reasons for union decline,
132; union membership, 4; union
structure, 57-58
Australian Council of Trade Unions,
30-31, 58

Brazil: government-union relations,
42-43; union federations, 42-43,
78-79

Canada: government-union relations,
31; membership in major unions,
17-18; public opinion about unions,
114; union structure, 59-60
Canadian Labor Congress, 31, 59-60
Chile: government-union relations,
43-44; union federations, 40-44,

Chile *(continued)*
79-80; union membership, 5
Codetermination, 63, 64, 151
Collective bargaining: Italy, 64;
Spain, 71; Sweden, 73

Danish Trade Union Federation, 32,
60-61; political alliance, 61
Denmark: government-union relations 31-32; union structure, 60-61

Earnings: developing countries, 138;
increase in real, 22; manufacturing, 21-22; union levels, 135-136
Economic growth rates, 13-14
Egypt: government-union relations,
44-45; union federations, 80; union
membership, 5
Employer associations: Australia,
94; Denmark, 31, 61, 92; France,
95; Germany, 94; India, 106; Italy,
96; Japan, 99; Kenya, 109; Malaysia, 104; New Zealand, 95; Norway,
92-93; Philippines, 105; Spain, 97;
Sweden, 93; Thailand, 105; United
Kingdom, 98
Employer-union relations: Australia,
94; Brazil, 107-108; Canada, 97;

ABOUT THE AUTHOR

WALTER GALENSON is Jacob Schurman Professor Emeritus at Cornell University, where he presently teaches in the graduate program in New York City. He has authored 39 articles and 13 books, and edited 9 other books on economics and related subjects.